The
CROSS
of
JESUS

Other titles by Warren W. Wiersbe (selected)

The CROSS —*of*— JESUS

What His Words from Calvary Mean for Us

Warren W. Wiersbe

 Baker Books

A Division of Baker Book House Co
Grand Rapids, Michigan 49516

© 1997 by Warren W. Wiersbe

Published by Baker Books
a division of Baker Book House Company
P.O. Box 6287, Grand Rapids, MI 49516-6287

Second printing, April 2000

Printed in the United States of America

Library of Congress Cataloging-in-Publication Data

Wiersbe, Warren W.
    The Cross of Jesus : what His words from Calvary mean for us / Warren W. Wiersbe.
        p.   cm.
    ISBN 0-8010-5781-7 (pbk.)
    1. Jesus Christ—Seven last words. I. Title.
BT456.W54   1997
232.96'35—dc21   97-15081

For information about academic books, resources for Christian leaders, and all new releases available from Baker Book House, visit our web site:
http://www.bakerbooks.com

CONTENTS

PREFACE

The focus of this book is on Jesus and the cross, and it covers four main topics:

What Jesus saw in the cross (chapter 1)
Why Jesus died on the cross (chapters 2–4)
What Jesus said from the cross (chapters 5–11)
How believers should live by the cross (chapter 12)

Chapters 5 to 11 were originally given as messages over "Back To The Bible Broadcast," and were published by The Good News Broadcasting Association, Lincoln, Nebraska. I have rewritten the messages and expanded them for this volume; however, I have retained their original informal style and evangelistic emphasis.

The remaining chapters were written especially for this book.

On Sunday evening, February 19, 1882, Charles Haddon Spurgeon opened his message with these words: "On whatever subjects I may be called to preach, I feel it to be a duty which I dare not neglect to be continually going back to the doctrine of the cross—the fundamental truth of justification by faith which is in Christ Jesus."

Unless we go back to the cross, we can't go forward in our Christian life. I trust that these simple studies will help you better understand the practical application of the death of Christ for your life and service today.

Warren W. Wiersbe

Unless otherwise noted, all Scripture quotations are from The New King James Version.

PART 1

What Jesus Saw in the Cross

WHEN JESUS LOOKED AT THE CROSS

Was it God's intention from the beginning that Jesus should go to the Cross?" asked the popular British preacher Dr. Leslie Weatherhead (1893–1976). "I think the answer to that question must be 'No.' I don't think Jesus thought that at the beginning of his ministry. He came with the intention that men should follow him, not kill him."[1]

But the Scriptures make it clear that the cross of Christ was neither a divine afterthought nor a human accident, for Jesus was "the Lamb slain from the foundation of the world" (Rev. 13:8). [2] In his message on the Day of Pentecost, Peter affirmed this truth when he said that Jesus was "delivered by the determined counsel and foreknowledge of God" (Acts 2:23). Peter was there when it happened; he knew that Calvary didn't catch Jesus by surprise. Years later, when he penned his first epistle, Peter called Jesus the Lamb that "was foreordained before the foundation of the world" (1 Peter 1:20). Could anything be clearer?

Paul agreed with Peter that the cross was in the mind and heart of God from the beginning. After all, if God promised eternal life "before time began" (Titus 1:2), and if he "chose us in him [Christ] before the foundation of the world" (Eph. 1:4) and wrote our names in the Book of Life (Rev. 17:8), then the great plan of salvation belongs to the divine counsels of eternity.

When Jesus came to earth, he knew that he came to die; so let's listen to the Master himself as he explained the Scriptures to those two discouraged disciples on the road to Emmaus. "Ought not the Christ to have suffered these things and to enter into His glory?" he asked (Luke 24:26). The cross was a divine assignment, not a human accident; it was a God-given obligation, not a human option. Later that same evening, Jesus appeared to the eleven apostles and said, "Thus it is written, and thus it was necessary for the Christ to suffer and to rise from the dead on the third day" (Luke 24:46). Jesus was not murdered; he willingly laid down his life for his sheep (John 10:15–18). His death was a necessity in the eternal plan of God.

i

The atoning sacrifice of the Messiah was taught in the Old Testament prophecies and types, and Jesus perfectly understood the Jewish Scriptures. The entire Mosaic sacrificial system, and the priesthood that maintained it, were types and shadows of the good things to come. Jesus knew what every Jew knew, that the heart of that system was Leviticus 17:11, "For the life of the flesh is in the blood, and I have given it to you upon the altar to make atonement for your souls; for it is the blood that makes atonement for the soul."

In his "birth announcement," Jesus declared that his incarnation gave to him a body that he would offer as a sacrifice for the sins of the world.

Therefore, when he came into the world, he said:

Sacrifice and offering You did not desire, but a body You have prepared for Me. In burnt offerings and sacrifices for sin You had no pleasure. Then I said, "Behold, I have come—in the volume of the book it is written of Me—to do Your will, O God." (Heb. 10:5–7)

Jesus would give himself as the burnt offering, in total surrender to God, as well as the sin offering to pay the price for our offenses against God. "Sacrifice" refers to any of the animal offerings and would include the trespass offering and the peace offering (see Lev. 1–7), while the word "offering" refers to the meal and drink offerings. By his death on the cross, Jesus fulfilled the entire sacrificial system and put an end to it forever. He accomplished with one offering what millions of animals on Jewish altars could never accomplish, "for it is not possible that the blood of bulls and goats could take away sins" (Heb. 10:4).

The sacrificial death of Christ was first publicly announced by John the Baptist when he saw Jesus coming to the Jordan River: "Behold! The Lamb of God who takes away the sin of the world!" (John 1:29, 36). John was answering Isaac's question, "Where is the lamb for the burnt offering?" (Gen. 22:7) and announcing the fulfillment of Abraham's promise, "My son, God will provide for Himself the lamb for a burnt offering" (Gen. 22:8).

Then John pictured his sacrificial death when he baptized Jesus in the Jordan River (Matt. 3:13–17; Mark 1:9–11; Luke 3:21–23; John 1:19–34), although only Jesus understood it at the time. John knew that Jesus wasn't a sinner needing to repent, so he hesitated to baptize him; but

Jesus knew that his baptism was the Father's will. "Permit it to be so now," he said to John, "for thus [in this manner] it is fitting for us to fulfill all righteousness" (Matt. 3:15).

We read these words casually, but they raise some difficult questions. To whom does the pronoun "us" refer? Does it include John? If it does, then we have a problem explaining how a sinful man could help a holy God "fulfill all righteousness." One solution is to forget John and note that the entire Godhead was involved in this important event. God the Father spoke from heaven; God the Son went into the water; and God the Holy Spirit descended upon Jesus as a dove. Doesn't this suggest that "us" refers to the Trinity—Father, Son and Holy Spirit? Isn't it God who fulfills all righteousness by giving his Son as a sacrifice for the sins of the world?

The New American Standard Bible translates Matthew 3:15 "for in this way it is fitting for us to fulfill all righteousness." In what way? In the way illustrated by his baptism: death, burial, and resurrection. In fact, Jesus used baptism as a picture of his passion: "But I have a baptism to be baptized with, and how distressed I am till it is accomplished" (Luke 12:50). He also identified himself with the experience of Jonah (Matt. 12:38–40; Luke 11:30), and again we see the image of death, burial, and resurrection.

In other words, as Jesus began his public ministry, he gave witness of the fact that he had come to die for the sins of the world. The only sign he would give to the Jewish nation was the same sign God sent to the wicked Ninevites: death, burial, and resurrection.

ii

The sacrificial lamb is the first of several vivid pictures of the death of Christ that are found in the Gospel of John. The second is the destroyed temple: "Destroy this temple, and in three days I will raise it up" (John 2:19). As with so many of our Lord's metaphorical utterances, this statement was misunderstood by those who heard it. They didn't realize that "He was speaking of the temple of His body" (John 2:21). At our Lord's trial, some of the witnesses cited this statement as proof that Jesus was an enemy of the Jewish law (Matt. 26:59–61; Mark 14:57–59), but this absurd witness accomplished nothing.

The body that God had prepared for his Son was the temple of God, for the eternal Word had become flesh and "tabernacled among us" (John 1:14 literal translation). "For it pleased the Father that in him all the fullness should dwell" (Col. 1:19). "For in him dwells all the fullness of the Godhead bodily" (Col. 2:9). And yet the lawless hands of wicked men were laid on that holy temple, and they did to him whatever they pleased. They thought they could destroy the Prince of Life, but their attempts were futile.

Contemplating the sufferings of Jesus and the horrible things sinful men did to the temple of his body causes us to marvel at the sinfulness of man and the mercy of God. In the space of a few hours, the officers arrested him, bound him, led (or pushed) him from one place to another, whipped him, spat upon him, humiliated him, made him wear a painful crown of thorns, and then led him out to nail him to a cross. This was all done to a man who was absolutely innocent! In all of human history, never was there such a miscarriage of justice.

They tried to destroy this temple, but they failed. God fulfilled the promise of Psalm 16:10 that Peter quoted in his Pentecostal sermon: "For You will not leave my soul in Hades, nor will You allow Your Holy One to see corruption" (see Acts 2:25–28). Jesus triumphantly arose from the dead on the third day, and the sign of Jonah to Israel was completed.

John's third picture of the crucifixion is the uplifted serpent. Jesus told Nicodemus, "And as Moses lifted up the

15

serpent in the wilderness, even so must the Son of man be lifted up, that whoever believes in Him should not perish but have eternal life" (John 3:14–15). Nicodemus was familiar with the story recorded in Numbers 21:5–9, but he must have been shocked to learn that the promised Messiah would have to endure such an ignoble death. King David compared himself to a worm (Ps. 22:6), but how could the miracle-working teacher sent from God compare himself to a vile serpent? It was unthinkable!

That the Messiah must be "lifted up" on a cross also perplexed the common people who had been taught that their promised Redeemer would "remain forever" (John 12:32–34). To be hung on a tree was the ultimate humiliation; it was the same as being put under a curse, "for he who is hanged is accursed of God" (Deut. 21:22–23). But on the cross, Jesus was made a curse for us and thereby redeemed us from the curse of the law (Gal. 3:13).

iii

If considered by themselves, the images of the lamb, the temple, and the serpent might give us the false impression that in his death Jesus was a victim instead of the victor. This erroneous interpretation is balanced by the fourth image, that of the Good Shepherd (John 10:11–18) who willingly laid down his life for the sheep. Our Lord was not murdered against his will; he voluntarily gave himself to die for us. "Therefore My Father loves Me, because I lay down my life that I may take it again. No one takes it from me, but I lay it down of myself" (John 10:17–18).

If you were driving down the highway and saw a sheep on the road, you would feel sorry for the stupid animal and try to avoid hitting it. But if in saving the animal you knew you would cause an accident and kill a human being, you certainly would opt to save the human and sacrifice the animal. Even Jesus admitted that humans are of greater value than animals (Matt. 12:11). But Jesus, the Good Shepherd, was willing to give his life for sinners who deserved to die! "I am the good shepherd. The good shepherd gives His life for the sheep" (John 10:11).

Under the old covenant, the sheep died for the shepherd, but they did it ignorantly and unwillingly. It's doubtful that any sheep ever volunteered to have its throat cut and its body butchered and then burned on an altar. But the gospel message declares that Jesus, the Good Shepherd, willingly died for the lost sheep of the world and did it with full knowledge of all that was involved. He didn't die a martyr's death; he died a criminal's death on a shameful Roman cross. "He was numbered with the transgressors" (Isa. 53:12; Mark 15:28).

The fifth picture of his death is the seed buried in the ground to produce fruit (John 12:20–28). The emphasis is on Christ's willingness to give his life so that the Father might be glorified. "The hour has come that the Son of Man should be glorified. Most assuredly, I say to you, unless a grain of wheat falls into the ground and dies, it remains alone; but if it dies, it produces much grain" (John 12:23–24).

Our Lord's death and burial looked like defeat for God and victory for the enemy, but it was just the opposite. His seeming defeat was actually the greatest victory Jesus ever won, a far greater victory than healing the sick or casting out demons. Our Lord's body was like a dead seed when Nicodemus and Joseph placed it in the tomb, but on the third day it was resurrected in power and glory. Today the preaching of his gospel is producing fruit all over the world (Col. 1:5–6).

Here, then, are five pictures of our Lord's death on the cross, each of them emphasizing a particular truth. Like the lamb on the altar, Jesus died as a substitute for us who deserved to die. The Jewish priests were careful to give as little pain as possible to the animal being sacrificed, but Jesus' body was treated like a building being destroyed. It was a substitutionary death, a cruel death and a vile death, for he was like a serpent lifted up and made a curse. But his was a voluntary death, the Shepherd willingly dying for the sheep, the seed willingly being planted in the ground and producing new life.

At this point, all we can do is worship.

> Amazing love! How can it be
> That Thou, my God, shouldst die for me?
> (Charles Wesley)

iv

Our Lord didn't speak to his disciples openly about the cross until after Peter's confession of faith at Caesarea Philippi (Matt. 16:13–20). "From that time Jesus began to show to His disciples that He must go to Jerusalem, and suffer many things from the elders and chief priests and scribes, and be killed, and be raised the third day" (Matt. 16:21). This announcement stunned them, and Peter intensely opposed the idea. But Jesus rebuked him and told him and the other apostles that if they wanted to be his true disciples, they would have to deny themselves, take up their own crosses, and follow him (Matt. 16:22–28). There was a cross in Peter's future as well as in our Lord's future.

From that time on, Jesus "steadfastly set His face to go to Jerusalem" (Luke 9:51; and see 13:22, 33), knowing full well what kind of reception he would receive there. From time to time, he reminded the Twelve what would happen to him in the Holy City, but they were unable to grasp what he was talking about (Mark 9:9–10, 30–32; 10:32–34). His enemies understood his parable about the wicked tenants

(Matt. 21:33–46), but the disciples seemed to miss the point completely. So blind was Peter to the plan of God that he tried to defend Jesus when the officers arrested him in the Garden (Matt. 26:51–54). While we admire Peter's courage and unselfish devotion to the Master, we regret his disobedience in the light of all that Jesus had taught him and his associates about the purposes of God.

However, let's not be too eager to cast the first stone. After all, it's much easier for us to understand the meaning of our Lord's death since we live on the resurrection side of Calvary and have complete Bibles. The shadows disappear when you look at Calvary through the empty tomb. However, when it comes to the cross of Jesus Christ, there's still much more for us to learn and put into practice in daily life.

This much is certain: our Lord's vision of the cross was far different from that of his disciples. They saw it as defeat, but he saw it as victory. To them, it meant shame; to Jesus, it meant glory. To the people of that day, the cross meant weakness, but Jesus turned the cross into a thing of power. Paul understood this and wrote with his own hand, "But God forbid that I should boast except in the cross of our Lord Jesus Christ, by whom the world has been crucified to me, and I to the world" (Gal. 6:14).

PART 2

Why Jesus Died on the Cross

He Died That We Might Live through Him

In this the love of God was manifested toward us, that God has sent His only begotten Son into the world that we might live through Him. In this is love, not that we loved God, but that He loved us and sent His Son to be the propitiation for our sins" (1 John 4:9–10). The fundamental problem lost sinners face isn't that they're sick and need a remedy. The problem is that they're "dead in trespasses and sins" (Eph. 2:1) and need to experience resurrection. Religion and reformation may cosmetize the corpse and make it more presentable, but religion and reformation can never give life to the corpse. Only God can do that. "But God, who is rich in mercy, because of His great love with which He loved us, even when we were dead in trespasses, made us alive together with Christ" (Eph. 2:4–5). No doubt our Lord raised many people from the dead (Matt. 11:5), but in the Gospel records, only three persons' resurrections are described: Jairus's daughter (Luke 8:40–56), the son of a widow at Nain (Luke 7:11–17), and Lazarus, a special friend of Jesus (John 11). As you study these three resurrection accounts, you learn some basic truths about the spiritual resurrection that brings salvation and new life to those who believe on Jesus Christ.

i

Jairus's daughter was only twelve years old, but she died. The widow's son was "a young man," perhaps in his late teens or early twenties, but he died. We get the impression that Lazarus was an older man, but Lazarus died. If these three persons teach us anything, it's that death is no respecter of age, and since death is a picture of sin, these three persons teach us that sin has slain the whole human race. Children are sinners, young people are sinners, and adults are sinners. "For all have sinned and fall short of the glory of God" (Rom. 3:23).

Note also that there is a time element involved. When Jesus arrived at Jairus's house, the little girl had just died. The young man in the funeral procession out of Nain had been dead at least a day, for the Jews usually buried within twenty-four hours of death. Lazarus had been in the grave four days by the time Jesus arrived in Bethany (John 11:39). Question: Which of these persons was the most dead? You smile at that question, and rightly so; there are no degrees of death. However, there are degrees of decay. Jairus's daughter wasn't decayed at all; in fact, she looked like she was only asleep. Decay was just starting in the young man's body. As for Lazarus, Martha warned that after four days in the tomb, her brother smelled! While all lost sinners, whether young or old, are spiritually dead, not all are in the same state of decay. Some sinners are prodigal sons who smell of the pigpen, while others are Pharisees, respectably clean on the outside, but filled with corruption on the inside (Matt. 23:25–28).

When I served as senior pastor at the Moody Church in Chicago, I quickly discovered that the church sanctuary was in a unique location on that triangle where LaSalle Boulevard and Clark Street met. If I exited the building through a door on LaSalle Boulevard and walked west, I quickly found myself in "Old Town," a neighborhood that (at that time) was populated by runaway teens, people looking for "adult" bookstores, drunks, dope peddlers, and "drifters" of all varieties. However, if I exited to Clark Street and walked east, I found myself in what's known in Chicago as the "Gold Coast," a neighborhood quite different from "Old Town." Many of the people in the "Gold Coast" were cultured and well dressed and drove expensive automobiles. In nice weather, the society ladies walked their pedigreed poodles down clean sidewalks; in cooler weather, some of the poodles wore little sweaters. The point I'm making is this: whether you lived in "Old Town" with its moral and material poverty or in the "Gold Coast" with its culture and prosperity, if you didn't have faith in Jesus, you were spiritually dead. The only difference between the "Old Town" sinners and the "Gold Coast" sinners was the extent of decay. You could smell corruption in "Old Town"; but in the "Gold Coast," the smell of decay was cosmetized and covered by expensive cologne.[1] "For the wages of sin is death" (Rom. 6:23), and there are no degrees of death, only degrees of decay. The lost sinner who says, "Well, I'm not as bad as other people," is missing the point. The issue isn't decay; it's death.

ii

The thing a dead person needs most is life, and that life can come only from Jesus Christ. Spiritual life is a gift, just as physical life is a gift. You and I can *nurture* physical life, but we can't *give* life to someone who's dead. Only God can do that. "For as the Father has life in Himself, so He has granted the Son to have life in Himself" (John 5:26).

How does Jesus impart this gift of life? Through his Word. "Most assuredly I say to you, he who hears My word and believes in Him who sent Me has everlasting life, and shall not come into judgment, but has passed from death into life" (John 5:24). In each of the resurrection narratives we're examining, Jesus spoke to the dead person: "Young man, I say to you, arise" (Luke 7:14); "Little girl, arise" (Luke 8:54); "Lazarus, come forth!" (John 11:43). In each case, the living Word spoken with divine authority gave the dead person life. The Word of God possesses life. "For the word of God is living and powerful. . . ." (Heb. 4:12). Those who receive that Word by faith have been "born again, not of corruptible seed but incorruptible, through the word of God which lives and abides forever" (1 Peter 1:23). Even though they are dead in trespasses and sins, lost sinners can hear the voice of the Son of God as the Spirit of God uses the Word to declare their need and the grace of God that meets their need. "So then faith comes by hearing, and hearing by the word of God" (Rom. 10:17).

iii

We should note further that each of these three persons that Jesus raised from the dead gave trustworthy evidence before others that they were truly alive. The miracle took place before witnesses who were amazed at what Jesus did. When the new life came to Jairus's daughter, the little girl arose from her bed, walked around, and took some food (Mark 5:42–43; Luke 8:55). If the resurrection of the dead is an illustration of the spiritual resurrection of dead sinners, then all who trust Christ should give evidence of their new life by their walk and their appetite. The Christian's conduct—daily walk—is different because of the new life within. "Just as Christ was raised up from the dead by the glory of the Father, even so we also should walk in newness of life" (Rom. 6:4). "If then you were raised with Christ, seek those things which are above, where Christ is, sitting at the right hand of God. Set your mind on things above, not on things on the earth" (Col. 3:1–2; and see Eph. 4:17–24). With the coming of the new nature within (2 Peter 1:3–4), the child of God receives a new appetite for the things of God. Like newborn babes, we desire the food of God's Word (1 Peter 2:2–3), and we won't settle for substitutes. We recognize the voice of the Good Shepherd, the voice that raised us from the dead, and we'll not follow counterfeits (John 10:4–5, 27–30). Only the Good Shepherd can lead us into the green pastures of his Word and nourish us with the truth that satisfies us within. "Your words were found, and I ate them, and Your word was to me the joy and rejoicing of my heart; for I am called by Your name, O Lord God of hosts" (Jer. 15:16).

The young man gave evidence that he was alive by sitting up and speaking (Luke 7:15). Surely if there's new life within us, it will be revealed by what we say and how we say it. If the heart is changed through faith in Christ, then the speech must also be changed: "For out of the abundance of the heart the mouth speaks" (Matt. 12:34). For one thing, the new life will reveal itself by our speaking truth instead of lies. "Therefore, putting away lying, 'Let each one of you speak truth with his neighbor,' for we are members of one another" (Eph. 4:25). That's the positive admonition; the negative is in Colossians 3:9, "Do not lie to one another, since you have put off the old man with his deeds." No more deception! Our speech will also be gracious, pure, kind, and loving. "But now you must put off all these: anger, wrath, malice, blasphemy, filthy language out of your mouth" (Col.

3:8). "Let your speech be always with grace, seasoned with salt, that you may know how you ought to answer each one" (Col. 4:6). "Let all bitterness, wrath, anger, clamor, and evil speaking be put away from you, with all malice" (Eph. 4:31). "Remind them . . . to speak evil of no one, to be peaceable, gentle, showing all humility to all men" (Titus 3:1–2). No more verbal abuse! Certainly our new speech will magnify the Lord Jesus Christ. It's likely that the young man never stopped telling people about Jesus and what he had done for him. "Come and hear, all you who fear God, and I will declare what He has done for my soul" (Ps. 66:16). "For we cannot but speak the things which we have seen and heard" (Acts 4:20). No more self-centered conversation!

Lazarus gave proof that he was alive by coming to the door of the tomb, even though he was bound hand and foot, and then being loosed from the graveclothes (John 11:44). Why would a living person want to be bound like a corpse and smell like a corpse? The apostle Paul may have had Lazarus in mind when he told the Ephesian believers to "put off, concerning your former conduct, the old man which grows corrupt according to the deceitful lusts, and be renewed in the spirit of your mind, and . . . put on the new man which was created according to God, in true righteousness and holiness" (Eph. 4:22–24). People who have been resurrected through faith in Jesus Christ will want to put off the graveclothes and put on the "grace clothes" that identify the true child of God. "Do not lie to one another, since you have put off the old man with his deeds, and have put on the new man who is renewed in knowledge according to the image of Him who created him. . . . Therefore, as the elect of God, holy and beloved, put on tender mercies, kindness, humility, meekness, longsuffering; bearing with one another, and forgiving one another. . . ." (Col. 3:9–10, 12). There's no avoiding the fact that eternal life must reveal itself through the lives of those who have been raised from the dead by the power of God.

iv

Jesus Christ doesn't simply *have* life and *give* life; he *is* life. He said what nobody else can ever say, "I am the resurrection and the life" (John 11:25); "I am the way, the truth, and the life" (John 14:6). The apostle John wrote, "The life was manifested, and we have seen, and bear witness, and declare to you that eternal life which was with the Father and was manifested to us" (1 John 1:2). "In Him was life, and the life was the light of men" (John 1:4). That's why it's essential for sinners to trust Jesus Christ and receive him into their hearts, because only then can they have eternal life. "And this is the testimony: that God has given us eternal life, and this life is in His Son. He who has the Son has life; he who does not have the Son of God does not have life" (1 John 5:11–12). What a paradox: he died that we might have life! What a tragedy: this life is available to all who will receive Christ, yet so few will repent and believe. Or, it may be that we haven't told them the Good News.

He Died That We Might Live for Him

"For the love of Christ compels us, because we judge thus: that if One died for all, then all died; and He died for all, that those who live should live no longer for themselves, but for Him who died for them and rose again" (2 Cor. 5:14–15).

In spite of the kindness, altruism, and philanthropy demonstrated by many unsaved people, the person without Christ is basically selfish in all that he or she does, as is the person who knows Christ but doesn't live for him. "For we ourselves were also once foolish, disobedient, deceived, serving various lusts and pleasures, living in malice and envy, hateful and hating one another" (Titus 3:3). Even our acts of so-called goodness to others were tinged with selfishness and self-gratification, so that nothing we did could ever meet God's high standard of righteousness. Whether we admitted it or not, our desire was to please ourselves, not to glorify the Lord.

The reason, of course, is because we were mastered by the world, the flesh, and the devil (Eph. 2:1–3). We lived "according to the course of this world," that invisible system around us that hates Christ and wants to pressure us into conformity with its evil ways (Rom. 12:2). We were subtly energized by "the prince of the power of the air." We were disobedient to God and yet thought we were free to do whatever we pleased. Our desire was to gratify "the lusts of our flesh," forgetting that sin ultimately has terrible consequences.

But now we have a new Master! We no longer live for ourselves but for the Savior who gave himself for us on the cross. Because we've come to the cross and trusted Jesus Christ, we've been set free—redeemed—from the bondage of the old life. When Jesus died on the cross, he defeated every evil master that controlled our life—the world, the flesh, and the devil.

Let's begin with "the world," that Satan-directed system of things that opposes God and his people. "But God forbid that I should glory except in the cross of our Lord Jesus Christ, by whom the world has been crucified to me, and I to the world" (Gal. 6:14). In his great victory on Calvary, Jesus defeated the world system so that it need not control us any longer. If, like Demas (2 Tim. 4:10), we love this present world, then we'll gradually go back into slavery, but if we're careful to obey 1 John 2:15–17, we'll experience victory.

On the cross Jesus also conquered the flesh. "And those who are Christ's have crucified the flesh with its passions and desires" (Gal. 5:24). How do we apply this victory to our own lives? The next verse tells us: "If we live in the Spirit, let us also walk in the Spirit" (v. 25). The New International Version translates it "let us keep in step with the Spirit." Only through the Holy Spirit can we identify personally with Christ's victory on the cross and appropriate it as our own.

Finally, on the cross Jesus defeated the devil. "Now is the judgment of this world; now the ruler of this world will be cast out. And I, if I am lifted up from the earth, will draw all peoples to Myself" (John 12:31–32). "Having disarmed principalities and powers, He made a public spectacle of them, triumphing over them in it [the cross]" (Col. 2:15). The battle Jesus fought on the cross against the powers of hell wasn't a minor skirmish; it was a major assault that ended in a complete victory for the Savior.

Since Jesus Christ is our new Master, "we make it our aim . . . to be well pleasing to Him" (2 Cor. 5:9). We know that one day we will give an account of our service when we stand at the judgment seat of Christ, and we want that account to glorify him (2 Cor. 5:10–11). We want to be able to say what Jesus said to his Father: "I have glorified You on the earth. I have finished the work which You have given Me to do" (John 17:4).

ii

Not only do we have a new Master, but we also have a new motive: "For the love of Christ compels us. . . ." (2 Cor. 5:14).

It was love that motivated the Father to give his Son to be the Savior of the world (John 3:16; Rom. 5:8; 1 John 4:9–10), and it was love that motivated the Son to give his life for the sins of the world (John 15:13). Paul exclaimed, "[He] loved me and gave Himself for me" (Gal. 2:20). No wonder John wrote, "Behold what manner of love [what foreign kind of love] the Father has bestowed on us, that we should be called children of God!" (1 John 3:1).

However, keep in mind that God not only loved the lost world, but he also loved his Son. The first time you read the word "love" in the New Testament is when the Father declares from heaven, "This is My beloved Son" (Matt. 3:17). In fact, the first time you read the world "love" in the Bible is when God spoke of Abraham's love for his only son and then commanded him to sacrifice his son on the altar (Gen. 22). "The Father loves the Son" (John 3:35; 5:20), and yet the Father was willing to give his beloved Son as a sacrifice for our sins on the cross.

> Amazing love! How can it be?
> That Thou my God should'st die for me!
> (Charles Wesley)

But the love that motivates our lives isn't something that we manufacture in our own strength. Rather, it's the gift of God to us by his Spirit. "The love of God has been poured out in our hearts by the Holy Spirit who was given to us" (Rom. 5:5). As we "keep in step with the Spirit," he produces the fruit of the Spirit in our lives, and the first-named fruit in that list is "love" (Gal. 5:22). This includes love for God, love for God's people, love for a lost world, and even love for our enemies.

Never underestimate the power of God's love in the life of a dedicated believer. It's the secret of bearing burdens, fighting battles, and overcoming barriers to get the job done that God has given us to do. No amount of money or other earthly reward would even tempt God's servants to do what love compels them to do. "If Jesus Christ be God and died for me," said missionary C. T. Studd as he headed for Africa, though he was ill and had been warned not to go, "then no sacrifice can be too great for me to make for Him."

iii

Because of the cross of Christ, we live by a new measure. We don't look at other people the way we did when we were

33

lost. "Therefore, from now on, we regard no one according to the flesh" (2 Cor. 5:16).

How do you view a lost world? What do you see in your heart when you watch unsaved people acting like unsaved people? Do they irritate you, repel you, make you angry? When Jesus looked at lost sinners, he saw them as helpless and harassed sheep, wandering hopelessly without a shepherd. He was moved with compassion by what he beheld (Matt. 9:36). He also saw a waiting harvest that would become a wasted harvest if somebody didn't bring in the sheaves (Matt. 9:37–38; John 4:35–38). He saw sinners as diseased patients needing the remedy for sin which only the Great Physician could provide (Matt. 9:9–13).

Filled with pride and contempt, the Pharisees condemned sinners and criticized Jesus for paying attention to them (Luke 15:1–2), but compelled by compassion, Jesus welcomed sinners and even died for them on the cross. If our faith in Jesus Christ isolates us from those who need him, there's something wrong with our faith—and our love.

We live by a new measure. We value people, not for what they own or what they can do for us, but for what they can be when they trust Jesus Christ. "Therefore, if anyone is in Christ, he is a new creation; old things have passed away; behold, all things have become new" (2 Cor. 5:17). If we are really constrained by love, then we see every lost sinner we meet—including those who persecute us—as candidates for the new creation. The gospel is the Good News that we don't have to stay the way we are. People can be changed and become a part of the new creation!

It's tragic that so much of the measuring going on in our world is based on our first birth rather than our second birth. People are judged by their physical appearance, their race, their abilities, their wealth, their nationality, or family ties. This kind of measuring creates pride, competition, and division. "All men are created equal" is true as far as the law is concerned, but all people are not equal in other ways. Some are smarter than others, stronger than others, more gifted than others. To measure people from the human perspective rather than on the basis of what God says in his Word is to invite competition, pride, and division.

Love sees potential in people. Jesus said to Simon, "You are Simon the son of Jonah. You shall be called Cephas [a stone]" (John 1:42). Did any of Simon Peter's family or friends really believe that Simon was a stone? It made no difference; Jesus believed it and later proved that he was right!

Love always brings out the best in us and in others. Love never gives up on people, because love "bears all things, believes all things, hopes all things, endures all things" (1 Cor. 13:7). In spite of Peter's occasional lapses of faith, Jesus continued to love him and challenged him to grow. Peter finally came to realize that his love for Christ was the most important thing in his life. "Simon, son of Jonah, do you love Me more than these?" (John 21:15).

When we evaluate people, we tend to look on the outward appearance; the Lord looks on the heart. We investigate the past; Jesus anticipates the future. Both Moses and Jeremiah were certain that God was mistaken when he called them into his service, but God made them effective servants and proved both of them wrong. God called Gideon a "mighty man of valor" before that frightened farmer had ever led an army (Judg. 6:12), and Gideon became a mighty man of valor. God wasn't wrong about Moses and Jeremiah and Gideon, and he isn't wrong about you and me.

iv

Because we belong to the new creation, we live under a new mandate. God has given to us "the ministry of reconciliation" (2 Cor. 5:18) and that makes us "ambassadors for

Christ" (2 Cor. 5:20). As God's children, we're in this world to declare peace, not war, and to let people know that Jesus can put together everything that sin has torn apart. God has "reconciled us to Himself through Jesus Christ" (2 Cor. 5:18) so that we're able to share his love and peace in a broken world filled with shattered people.

Because of the cross, God is reconciling rebellious sinners with himself through Jesus Christ. Through his people, he pleads, "Be reconciled to God!" (2 Cor. 5:20). "And the Spirit and the bride say, 'Come!' And let him who hears say, 'Come!' And let him who thirsts come. Whoever desires, let him take the water of life freely" (Rev. 20:17). The Spirit, through the church, is convicting the world and calling lost sinners back to God.

God is not only reconciling lost sinners to himself, but he's also reconciling believers to one another. Believing Jews and Gentiles are made one in Christ, members of the same body, citizens of the same household of faith, living stones in the same glorious temple (Eph. 2:11–22). The "first birth" differences, which bring division and competition in the world, don't divide the church of the twice born, for "there is neither Jew nor Greek, there is neither slave nor free, there is neither male nor female; for you are all one in Christ Jesus" (Gal. 3:28).

It's likely that the local churches in Paul's day were the only assemblies in the Roman Empire that welcomed everybody regardless of race, color, education, or social status. Wealthy patrons and poor slaves shared the same Lord's Supper, worshiped the same God, and listened to the same Scriptures. No one was rejected who was truly in Jesus Christ and a part of the new creation. "Now all who believed were together, and had all things in common" (Acts 2:44).

How do we carry on this vital "ministry of reconciliation" in today's splintered world? It begins with our example of love, for if people don't see the saints loving one another, how can they believe that God loves the sinners? The unity of the church in the Spirit and in love is the most powerful evangelistic tool we have.

"I do not pray for these alone," said Jesus, "but also for those who will believe in Me through their word; that they all may be one, as You, Father, are in Me, and I in You; that they also may be one in Us, that the world may believe that You sent Me. . . . I in them, and You in Me; that they may be made perfect in one, and that the world may know that You have sent Me, and have loved them as You have loved Me" (John 17:20–21, 23).

This spiritual unity Jesus prayed for isn't something invisible, seen only by God. It's a visible unity that the world can see as Christians love one another and thereby prove themselves to be Christ's disciples (John 13:34–35). Jesus wasn't asking the Father to put all the churches and denominations together into one "world church" but to bind all true Christians together in love regardless of their local affiliations. It wasn't a church of diluted doctrine or compromised convictions, for "the unity of the faith" is as important as our unity in love (Eph. 4:11–13). We're supposed to love the truth as well as love one another (1 Cor. 13:6; 2 Thess. 2:10).

When we live in this atmosphere of love and unity, it's much easier for us to share Christ with the lost, to pray for them, and to do the kind of good works that glorify God (Matt. 5:16). We can't reach and change the whole world, but we can bear witness in our own personal world where God has placed us. Mary of Bethany gave her best to Jesus right where she was, and for centuries what she did has touched people around the world (Matt. 26:13; Mark 14:9). If you want to live for Jesus, don't dream about faraway places and exciting new experiences. Start right where you are and let God guide you the rest of the way.

He Died That We Might Live with Him

For God did not appoint us to wrath, but to obtain salvation through our Lord Jesus Christ, who died for us, that whether we wake or sleep, we should live together with Him. (1 Thess. 5:9–10)

Paul was writing about heaven, the glorious home of every child of God, for one of the purposes behind our Lord's death was that we might live eternally with him.

i

The brilliant mathematician and philosopher Alfred North Whitehead (1861–1947) once said to a friend, "As for the Christian theology, can you imagine anything more appallingly idiotic than the Christian idea of heaven?"[1] But Christian believers, including many intelligent theologians, don't consider the heaven described in the Bible to be "appallingly idiotic," nor did Jesus Christ, who knew more about the subject than anybody. If Dr. Whitehead had known the Bible as well as he knew Plato and Aristotle, he probably wouldn't have made that statement.

Heaven was real to Jesus "who for the joy that was set before Him endured the cross, despising the shame, and has sat down at the right hand of the throne of God" (Heb. 12:2). It was his vision of heaven that kept him going when the going was difficult. Centuries before, the assurance of heaven encouraged Abraham, Isaac, and Jacob. They kept their eyes on that future city and country that God was preparing for them (Heb. 11:13–16).

This morning I read the obituary of a man in our city who felt ill on Friday, visited his doctor for blood tests and was immediately sent to the hospital, and died on Monday. When you realize the brevity of life and the finality of death, is it "appallingly idiotic" to want to know where you're going when you die? Jesus knew where he was going after his death on the cross. Likewise, if you trust him as your Savior, you can know where you are going.

Christians have been accused of being "so heavenly minded that they're no earthly good," and perhaps this is true of some. But C. S. Lewis wrote, "If you read history you will find that the Christians who did most for the present world were precisely those who thought most of the next. . . . It is since Christians have largely ceased to think of the other world that they have become so ineffective in this."[2] Knowing that we're going to heaven should make a difference in the way we live today.

The Christian's hope of heaven rests upon three unshakable pillars, the first of which is the promise that Jesus made: "In My Father's house are many mansions; if it were not so, I would have told you. I go to prepare a place for you. And if I go and prepare a place for you, I will come again and receive you to Myself; that where I am, there you may be also" (John 14:2–3). This promise is so clear that it needs no explanation. It's the best medicine for a troubled heart!

The second pillar is the prayer that Jesus prayed: "Father, I desire that they also whom You gave Me may be with Me where I am, that they may behold My glory which you have given Me. . . ." (John 17:24). Since the Father always answers the prayers of his beloved Son (John 11:41–42), we can be sure that this one is being answered too. This assures us that every believer who dies immediately goes to heaven to behold the glory of the Lord.

The third pillar is the price that Jesus paid. Paul comforted the troubled Thessalonian believers, who were young in the faith, by telling them that whether they lived or died, Jesus would take them to heaven. That's why he died and rose again. When believers die, they go to be with Christ; "to be absent from the body" means "to be present with the Lord" (2 Cor. 5:6–8). If Jesus returns while we're still alive, then he will catch us up to meet him in the air and we will be with him forever (1 Thess. 4:14–18).

We want to focus on this third pillar—the price that Jesus paid—and discover the relationship between the cross of Christ and heaven.

ii

Little children get homesick, but adults experience "culture shock." The term "culture shock" is a familiar one to us today, but it was a new concept back in 1940 when it first appeared in print. If you've ever traveled in unfamiliar territory, especially in a foreign country, you may have wrestled with the emotional trauma that can come when you're "out of your element." But consider what it meant for the Son of God to come to earth from heaven, to live among sinful people and then to die on a cross. Talk about "culture shock"!

He came from the harmonies of heaven into the discords of earth, from holiness and glory to sinfulness and shame, taking upon himself a body in which he would experience the normal trials of humanity: weariness, hunger, thirst, physical and emotional suffering, and eventually death.

This isn't to say that in the days of his flesh Jesus had no joys, because he did. Though he was "a man of sorrows and acquainted with grief" (Isa. 53:3), he was still able to say to his disciples before he went to the cross, "These things I have spoken to you, that My joy may remain in you, and that your joy may be full" (John 15:11). But during his ministry, Jesus was indeed "acquainted with grief," especially during his trial and crucifixion, for no one ever suffered as did the Son of God.

Certainly hell was at the cross of Calvary, motivating ignorant people to mock him and kill him. "Many bulls have surrounded Me," said David in Psalm 22, speaking prophetically about the Messiah, "strong bulls of Basham have encircled me. . . . For dogs have surrounded Me; the congregation of the wicked has enclosed Me" (vv. 12, 16). Paul tells us that the hosts of hell attacked our Lord while he was hanging on the cross. "Having disarmed principalities and powers, He made a public spectacle of them, triumphing over them in it [the cross]" (Col. 2:15). The spectators at Calvary saw neither the battle nor the victory, but the hosts of heaven and hell watched with interest and concern and saw Jesus conquer.

As terrible as the cross was, we must remember that heaven was there as well as hell. Jesus was on the cross fulfilling his Father's will, drinking the cup his Father had prepared for him. Wherever you find somebody doing God's will, that place is an outpost of heaven. A small group of disciples gathered at the cross, which meant God was there with them: "For where two or three are gathered together in My name, I am there in the midst of them" (Matt. 18:20).

41

Every statement Jesus made from the cross was a word from heaven, fulfilling prophecy and giving encouragement. His prayer for the Father's forgiveness, his care for Mary, and especially his promise to the believing thief—"Assuredly, I say to you, today you will be with Me in Paradise" (Luke 23:43)—were all evidences that heaven was very near.

Close to the end of his ordeal, Jesus was forsaken by the Father and announced this fact in a loud voice: "My God, My God, why have You forsaken Me?" (Matt. 27:46). This was the climax of the awful darkness that had shrouded the cross for three hours. But shortly after that, he cried, "Father, into Your hands I commend My spirit" (Luke 23:46), proving that the Father and the Son were together again. He was forsaken by the Father that we might never be forsaken by God.

On that terrible day when Jesus died on the cross, heaven wasn't in the Jewish temple or in the city of Jerusalem, for Jesus had already passed sentence on the unbelieving nation: "See! Your house is left to you desolate" (Matt. 23:38). He wrote "Ichabod" over the city: "the glory has departed" (see 1 Sam. 4:19–22). Heaven wasn't in the Jewish Passover celebration; when the Lamb of God was sacrificed for the sins of the world, the Passover became an empty ritual whose real meaning could be found only in the Jesus the religious leaders had rejected.

Heaven's love and heaven's purposes brought Jesus to the cross and kept Jesus on the cross: "who for the joy that was set before him endured the cross" (Heb. 12:2). What was that joy? It was the joy of returning to the Father and having restored to him the glory he had laid aside at his incarnation (John 17:5). But this joy also includes sharing his glory with us when he presents his bride to the Father (Jude 24). Then his church will reign forever with him "to the praise of the glory of His grace" (Eph. 1:6).

Religion that rejects the cross is both impotent and ignorant, for the Christ of the cross is "the power of God and the wisdom of God" (1 Cor. 1:24). Only the Christ of the cross can bring us to God. Respectable religion that rejects the blood of the cross can't understand the message of the Bible, and it is powerless to deal with sin and sinful human nature. "Comfortable religion" that avoids bearing the cross and following Jesus is but a religious facade that knows nothing of true discipleship.

Heaven was at the cross because the cross is the only way to heaven. The way to God was opened, not by the life of Jesus or the example of Jesus, not even by the teaching of Jesus, but by the death of Jesus on the cross. "For Christ also suffered once for sins, the just for the unjust, that He might bring us to God. . . ." (1 Peter 3:18). We have "boldness to enter the holiest by the blood of Jesus" (Heb. 10:19).

> Not all the blood of beasts,
> On Jewish altars slain,
> Could give the guilty conscience peace,
> Or wash away the stain.
> But Christ the heavenly Lamb,
> Takes all our sins away;
> A sacrifice of nobler name
> And richer blood than they.
>
> (Isaac Watts)

iii

Heaven was at the cross, but the cross is also in heaven. Not the literal tree on which Jesus died, of course, but the cross is there just the same.

Let's begin with the wounds in the body of Jesus, the glorified body in which he ascended to heaven. Poets and hymn writers like to use the word "scars," perhaps because it's easier to rhyme, but the Scriptures know nothing of scars on the body of Jesus. When John saw the glorified Christ in heaven, he saw "a Lamb as though it had been slain" (Rev. 5:6, 9, 12). He saw wounds.

When God's people see Jesus and receive their glorified bodies, that will be the end of their own weakness, pain, disfigurement, disease, decay, and death. But when our Lord returned to glory, he chose to take his wounds with him—glorified wounds, to be sure—but wounds nonetheless. The only works of sinful man in heaven today are the wounds on the body of Jesus. But those wounds speak of sins forgiven and the sacrifice accepted. As he ministers as our High Priest and Advocate before the throne of God, Jesus does so as the slain Lamb of God. When Satan accuses the saints, the Son of God silences him with the prints of the nails and the wound of the spear in his side.

> Depth of mercy!
> Can there be Mercy still reserved for me?
> Can my God His wrath forbear—
> Me, the chief of sinners spare?
> There for me the Saviour stands,
> Holding forth His wounded hands;
> God is love! I know, I feel—
> Jesus weeps and loves me still.
>
> (Charles Wesley)

The cross is seen in heaven through the wounds of the Savior, but it's heard in heaven through the praises of the heavenly worshipers. In Revelation 4, the heavenly hosts sing about the Creator; in Revelation 5, their praise is about the Redeemer. "You are worthy to take the scroll, and to open its seals; for You were slain, and have redeemed us to God by Your blood out of every tribe and tongue and people and nation. . . ." (Rev. 5:9).

"If you want to attract people to your services," some contemporary church experts advise, "avoid using songs about the cross and the blood. The modern generation just doesn't grasp that kind of teaching or symbolism." But if you leave out the cross and the blood of Jesus, how can you preach the gospel message? If you preach Christ, you have to preach the cross ("Christ died for our sins"); if you don't preach a crucified Christ, you aren't preaching the gospel. And how can you preach from the Bible if you fail to tell sinners that he died "according to the Scriptures" (1 Cor. 15:3)? Since the hosts of heaven are praising the Lamb that was slain, why should the hosts on earth be silent about his death? The only way sinners can be saved is through the blood of the Lamb. The angels in heaven rejoice over every sinner that repents (Luke 15:7, 10). The angels must weep when they behold God's people who gather to worship Christ without speaking about his blood.

The Jewish high priest could enter the Holy of Holies only if he brought with him the blood of the sacrifice (Lev. 16), and no sinner can be cleansed and come into the presence of God apart from the blood of Jesus Christ (Heb. 10:19–25). Throughout all eternity, Jesus Christ will be praised as "the Lamb who was slain," and because of that praise, the cross will eternally be in heaven.

The very name of Jesus—the Lamb—helps to keep the cross central in heaven. In the Book of Revelation alone, Jesus is called "the Lamb" at least twenty-eight times. God's wrath is "the wrath of the Lamb" (Rev. 6:16); cleansing is by "the blood of the Lamb" (7:14); and the church is "the bride of the Lamb" (Rev. 19:7; 21:9). For all eternity, Jesus wants to be known as the Lamb!

iv

Jesus died that we might live *through* him, which is salvation; that we might live *for* him, which is dedication; and that we might live *with* him, which is glorification. No matter how difficult our pilgrim path may be here on earth, we know that we "will dwell in the house of the LORD forever" (Ps. 23:6).

"You will soon be leaving the land of the living," a pastor said to a dying saint, to which the man replied, "No, I'm not leaving the land of the living. I'm leaving the land of the dying and going to the land of the living!"

He was right. And he was able to give that good confession because he had been to the cross and been saved by the blood of Jesus Christ.

But not everybody is going to heaven. There's another place and it's called hell. Hell is the place where people go who have never trusted Jesus Christ as their Savior. Jesus described hell as a furnace of fire (Matt. 13:42, 50), and the apostle John (the apostle of love) called hell "a lake of fire" (Rev. 19:20; 20:10, 14–15; 21:8). Hell is a real place, just as heaven is a real place.

The cross of Christ is the only escape from eternal hell. The cross is also the greatest warning to lost sinners. Charles Spurgeon put it this way:

> The most terrible warning to impenitent men in all the world is the death of Christ. For if God spared not his own Son, on whom was only laid imputed sin, will he spare sinners whose sins are their own?[3]

But nobody has to go to hell. God is "not willing that any should perish, but that all should come to repentance" (2 Peter 3:9).

"We implore you on Christ's behalf, be reconciled to God. For He made Him who knew no sin to be sin for us, that we might become the righteousness of God in Him" (2 Cor. 5:20–21).

Part 3

What Jesus Said from the Cross

"Father, Forgive Them"

ast words can be very revealing. Like an X ray, they can expose the heart and mind of a person.

For example, what would you expect circus magnate P. T. Barnum to say on his deathbed? Probably just what he said: "What were today's receipts?" It's no surprise that Napoleon's last words were, "Chief of the army!" The great Baptist preacher Charles Spurgeon said as his last words, "Jesus died for me." John Wesley, the founder of Methodism, said, "The best of all is, God is with us."

On March 14, 1883, the day Karl Marx died, his housekeeper came to him and said, "Tell me your last words, and I'll write them down."

Marx replied, "Go on, get out! Last words are for fools who haven't said enough!"

Marx was wrong in that statement as he was in so many others. Jesus Christ had certainly said a great deal during his three short years of ministry on earth, and yet he thought it was important to say even more, and he said it from the place of suffering, the cross. The King of Kings turned the cross into a throne and spoke royal words of spiritual truth, words that we cherish and can still learn from even today. Since he is the truth and speaks the truth, whatever Jesus says is worthy of our consideration and meditation.

Our Lord's seven last words from the cross are important not only because of the person who spoke them, but also because of the place where they were said. While our Lord was doing his greatest work on earth, dying for the sins of the world, he uttered some of his greatest words. These seven last words from the cross are windows that enable us to look into eternity and see the heart of the Savior and the heart of the gospel.

The first of these seven statements is found in Luke 23:33–34:

> And when they had come to the place called Calvary, there they crucified Him, and the criminals, one on the right hand and the other on the left. Then Jesus said, "Father, forgive them; for they do not know what they do."

The Anguish

Coventry Cathedral in Coventry, England, is the most beautiful contemporary cathedral I have ever seen. My wife and I have visited it several times and are always overwhelmed by its splendor. When the morning sun comes through the recessed windows, you stand bathed in incredible beauty. The "Tablets of the Word" on the walls share the words of Jesus so vividly, you could use them to lead a sinner to faith in Christ.

The old cathedral was bombed the night of November 14, 1940, and its ruins still stand next to the new sanctuary, which was consecrated in 1962. To me, the most interesting thing about those ruins is the inscription carved on the wall behind the charred cross. The words simply say, "Father, forgive."

Father, forgive! This was the prayer of an anguished people who were watching their buildings being destroyed and their loved ones and friends being maimed and killed. Father, forgive! When you look at the ruins of the old cathedral, you can see a monument to man's selfishness and sin, but you can also see a memorial to the grace of God that enables Christians to pray for their enemies. "Father, forgive!"

Sometimes it's very difficult for us to forgive people. It's easier for us to harbor an unforgiving spirit, quite contrary to what the Bible teaches about forgiveness. Someone hurts us, and in our hearts we can't forgive or forget. Of course, in doing this we only hurt ourselves and keep the wound open, but there's something in human nature that loves to nurture a grudge. That's why we need to listen to Jesus pray, "Father, forgive them; for they do not know what they do" (v. 34).

These words are so familiar that we fail to notice how marvelous this statement really is. But if we grasp the wonder of this first word from the cross, it will enable us to forgive others and experience the joy that comes with true forgiveness.

The Address

Consider the wonder of the address. Jesus said, "Father." While he was on the cross, our Lord addressed God three times. His first statement was, "Father, forgive them; for they do not know what they do" (v. 34). The fourth and central statement was, "My God, my God, why have You forsaken me?" (Matt. 27:46). His final statement was, "Father, into Your hands I commit my spirit" (Luke 23:46).

His first words, his central words, and his last words were all directed to his Father. When our Lord entered into his suffering, when he was enduring suffering, and when he emerged victoriously from his suffering, he spoke to his Father in heaven. Nothing threatened his relationship with his Father.

In my pastoral ministry, I have sometimes heard people say, "I can't talk to God! I can't pray! The way people have treated me, I don't believe God cares anymore!" But look at the way people treated the Lord Jesus, the perfect Son of God! The religious leaders of his nation rejected him and asked for him to be crucified. His own disciples forsook him and fled. The soldiers treated him brutally, and Pilate declared him innocent—and then sent him to the cross! At one point, even the Father forsook his beloved Son; yet Jesus was able to look up and say, "Father."

Jesus lived in perfect fellowship with his Father. When Jesus began his ministry, the Father said, "This is my beloved Son, in whom I am well pleased" (Matt. 3:17). The Father and the Son enjoyed a fellowship of love, and Jesus was able to say, "I do always those things that please him" (John 8:29). But in the midst of terrible suffering, Jesus didn't fight his Father's will or question his Father's love.

When you and I are hurting, whether it's physical or emotional pain, we're tempted to say, "I wonder if God really loves me. I wonder if he cares." We know the answer. He does love us; he does care; he always will love us and care for us. God's holy character is much greater than our feelings, and his promises never fail. He's working out his purposes for us, even though he doesn't always explain his reasons.

How did Jesus turn trial into triumph? He prayed, "Father." When you can pray "Father," then the door opens for you to receive from your heavenly Father the power, grace, and help you need when you are suffering. It's not easy to suffer. Pain hurts. A broken heart hurts even more than a broken arm. But when you say "Father," then you can look up to heaven and know that the smile of God is upon you.

If you want to be able to forgive others, here is the place to start: be sure you have a right relationship with your Father in heaven. We can forgive our enemies because we know that the Father is in control and we have nothing to fear. In the place of prayer in the Garden, Jesus had willingly accepted the cup the Father prepared for him (John 18:10–11). Once you yield to the Father's will, you can receive from him the grace you need to forgive, then the wounds within can be healed.

The Appeal

Consider the wonder of the appeal: "Father, forgive them" (Luke 23:34). The tense of the verb "said" indicates that our Lord repeated this prayer. As the soldiers nailed him to the cross, he prayed, "Father, forgive them." When they lifted the cross and placed it in the hole in the ground, our Lord prayed, "Father, forgive them." As he hung there between heaven and earth, and heard religious people mocking him, he repeatedly prayed, "Father, forgive them."

Jesus could have prayed, "Father, judge them! Father, destroy them!" He could have called for legions of angels to deliver him, but he didn't. Many times you and I have wanted God to send fire from heaven on somebody who has hurt us, and we've prayed, "Father, judge them! Father, hurt them as they've hurt me!" But our Lord prayed from a heart of love, "Father, forgive them." What an example for us to follow!

What was Jesus accomplishing as he prayed this prayer?

The Fulfillment of God's Word

In Isaiah 53:12 (the great "Calvary chapter" of the Old Testament), you read these words: "Therefore I will divide Him a portion with the great, and He shall divide the spoil with the strong, because He poured out His soul unto death, and He was numbered with the transgressors, and He bore the sin of many, and made intercession for the transgressors." Our Lord Jesus Christ prayed for those who crucified him and fulfilled that Old Testament prophecy.

When we're suffering, most of us intercede for ourselves and not for others; Jesus forgot himself and thought of others. For God to forgive their sins was far more important than for God to remove his own Son's sufferings. Jesus had willingly yielded himself to die on the cross, so that important matter was already settled, but he wanted everybody to know that he forgave them for the way they treated him.

As well-versed as the scribes and rabbis were in the Old Testament Scriptures, you'd think one of them would have remembered Isaiah 53:12. Had they read the chapter in the Isaiah scroll, the Spirit of God could have opened their eyes to the truth about Messiah Jesus. But the scholars were too busy ridiculing him; they had no time to discover him in their own Scriptures.

He Practiced What He Taught Others

Jesus was not only fulfilling the Old Testament prophecy, but he was also practicing the truth that he taught to others. During his ministry, he both preached and practiced forgiveness. He said, "But if you do not forgive men their trespasses, neither will your Father forgive your trespasses" (Matt. 6:15). This doesn't mean that forgiveness is based on our own good works, or that we earn God's forgiveness by forgiving others. Nor does it suggest that Jesus needed forgiveness, because he was the spotless Lamb of God slain for the sins of the world (John 1:29; 1 Peter 1:18–19; 2:24). His prayer reminds us that if we're unwilling to forgive others, then our hearts are in no condition to ask God for his forgiveness. If I'm broken before God, then I'll be forgiving toward others.

We must remember that our Lord's death occurred during the time of the Roman Empire and the reign of Tiberius Caesar. Among their many deities, the Romans worshiped Justitia (Nemesis), the goddess of revenge and retribution (see Acts 28:1–6). Our Lord Jesus Christ did not worship revenge, nor should we. He prayed, "Father, forgive them," and in so doing fulfilled the Word and practiced his own message of forgiveness.

Only God can see the human heart, so only he knows the damage being done by people who will not forgive others. The virus of an unforgiving spirit has infected marriages, families, churches, and whole nations with devastating consequences. What a difference it would make if we would only learn to forgive and pray as Jesus prayed!

The Purpose of His Death

One reason Jesus died was that God might be able to freely forgive the sins of all who trust Christ. That's the message of the gospel: "Christ died for our sins" (1 Cor. 15:3). We don't have to carry the burden and guilt of sin because on Calvary Jesus bore the burden for us. Now we can be forgiven and we can be forgiving because of Calvary.

Our Lord said to the paralytic, "Man, your sins are forgiven you" (Luke 5:20). He said to the fallen woman who anointed him, "Your sins are forgiven" (Luke 7:48), then he added, "Go in peace" (7:50). Forgiveness is what the cross is all about. But though forgiveness is free, it is not cheap; it cost Jesus Christ his life.

You and I will have less of a problem forgiving others if we are right in our relationship with our Father and if we remember how much he has forgiven us for Jesus' sake. Those who don't forgive others tear down the very bridge on which they walk themselves. People have said to me, "But nobody knows how cruel other people have been to me." I remind them of how people treated the Lord Jesus; yet he was able to pray, "Father, forgive them; for they do not know what they do." Remember the wonder of this appeal and let it work in your own heart.

The Argument

There is a third wonder here, and it's the wonder of the argument our Lord gave to the Father as he prayed: "for they do not know what they do." Our Lord not only prayed for forgiveness for his enemies, but he even argued on their behalf! It's as though he stood as a lawyer and said to his Father, "Let me give you a reason why you should forgive them."

This statement has been greatly misunderstood. It doesn't mean that everybody is automatically forgiven because Jesus prayed this prayer. Nor does it mean that ignorance brings forgiveness. We all know that ignorance is no excuse in the sight of the law.

One day I was driving in Chicago and I made a simple left turn at an intersection I knew very well. Before long, I saw a flashing light behind me, so I pulled over to the curb. The police officer came over and said, "Sir, you made an illegal left turn." I had made that turn many times. Since the last time, however, the city had put up a "No Left Turn" sign there which I confessed I had not noticed.

I said, "Officer, I'm sorry, but I didn't know a left turn here had been made illegal." Do you know what he said to me? "Sir, that doesn't make any difference. You still broke the law." Ignorance is no excuse in the sight of the law.

Of what were these people ignorant?

They were ignorant of his person. In spite of their careful attention to the study of the Old Testament, the people didn't recognize their Savior and King when he arrived. They mocked him as a prophet and said, "Prophesy! Who is it that struck you?" (Luke 22:64). They mocked him as a king, putting a robe on him, giving him a scepter, and placing a crown of thorns on his head. They shouted to Pilate, "We have no king but Caesar!" (John 19:15). They laughed at Christ's claim that he was the Son of God. "He saved others; let Him save Himself if He is the Christ, the chosen of God" (Luke 23:35).

Why were they ignorant of his person? Because they refused to believe his Word and obey what he said. "If anyone wills to do [is willing to do] His will, he shall know concerning the doctrine, whether it is from God or whether I speak on My own authority" (John 7:17). Anyone who sincerely seeks to obey the truth of the Word will be led by the Spirit to confess that Jesus Christ is the Son of God. But the Jews were so locked into their traditional religious system that they wouldn't receive Christ's teaching and discover the reality of eternal life.

They were ignorant of the meaning of their own actions. They didn't realize that what they were doing was fulfilling their own Old Testament Scriptures. They parted his garments and cast lots for them (Luke 23:34), and that fulfilled Psalm 22:18. They gave him vinegar to drink (Luke 23:36), and that fulfilled Psalm 69:21. He was crucified between two transgressors (Luke 23:33), and that fulfilled Isaiah 53:12. Even his cry to the Father, "My God, my God, why have You forsaken Me?" is a quotation from Psalm 22:1, a psalm that the Jews certainly knew well.

The Romans and the Jews "by lawless hands" (Acts 2:23) put Jesus Christ to death, and yet their very actions fulfilled the plan of God. Even the wrath of man praises God (Ps. 76:10), and when sinners are doing their worst, God is giving his best.

They were ignorant of their own sin. The enormity of their sins never bothered them. They nailed the Son of God to a cross and then went about their business celebrating Passover! In the Old Testament, the law of Moses made provision for sins of ignorance but not for deliberate highhanded sins. The sin offering described in Leviticus 4 was for sins of ignorance that had been discovered and needed to be forgiven. In his prayer, Jesus said, "Father, My people don't understand; they are ignorant. They don't know what they're doing. Father, it's a sin of ignorance; so forgive them."

Does this suggest that ignorance will get a sinner into heaven without that sinner first trusting Jesus Christ? No, it doesn't! Certainly those who know the truth and have rejected it have a greater obligation before God than those who have never heard, but ignorance is not a substitute for repentance and faith. If it were, then the fewer people we tell about Jesus, the more people there will be in heaven!

Lost sinners are blind and don't realize what they're doing to themselves and to the Lord by hardening their hearts and refusing to repent. As Jesus said to Saul of Tarsus, "Saul, Saul, why are you persecuting Me? . . . It is hard for you to kick against the goads" (Acts 9:4–5). If lost sinners will humbly follow the light that God gives them, they'll eventually know the truth and be saved.

The Answer

What did this prayer accomplish? What was God's answer? God's answer was grace and mercy: judgment did not fall. God continued to send his message of salvation to the very nation that had crucified his Son. The apostle Peter told the Jewish leaders, "I know that you did it [crucified Jesus] in ignorance, as did also your rulers" (Acts 3:17). God was patient with Israel and gave them nearly forty years of grace before the city of Jerusalem was destroyed by the Romans in 70 A.D.

The apostle Paul wrote concerning the sins of his own preconversion days, "I obtained mercy because I did it ignorantly in unbelief" (1 Tim. 1:13). In answer to Christ's prayer, God was patient with Saul of Tarsus. Many people in Jerusalem did come to know Christ as Savior, including Saul of Tarsus who became the great apostle Paul.

God doesn't always judge sin immediately. In his mercy, he postpones his judgment because his Son prayed, "Father, forgive them; for they do not know what they do." You and

I are living in a day of grace, not a day of judgment. It's a day when God is seeking to reconcile lost sinners to himself in answer to his Son's wonderful prayer. Today God will forgive any sinner who repents and turns by faith to Jesus Christ.

Charles Wesley wrote in one of his hymns:

> Five bleeding wounds He bears
> Received on Calvary;
> They pour effectual prayers,
> They strongly plead for me,
> "Forgive him, O forgive," they cry,
> "Nor let that ransomed sinner die."

"Father, forgive them; for they do not know what they do."

The Promise of Paradise

Whenever a lost sinner repents of sin and trusts Jesus Christ as Savior, that person is born into God's family and immediately becomes a child of God. "But as many as received Him, to them He gave the right to become children of God, to those who believe in His name" (John 1:12).

Salvation is really an amazing experience because when you believe on Jesus a miracle takes place. The spiritually dead sinner is raised to eternal life and is brought from darkness to light. The Bible calls this experience a "new birth" (John 3), receiving the divine life and the divine nature within.

For each believer, the miracle of the new birth is the same, but the circumstances surrounding that miracle are different. Some conversion experiences are more marvelous than others. When I trusted Christ as my Savior, I was standing at the back of a high school auditorium listening to Billy Graham preach the gospel. I didn't raise my hand for prayer nor did I walk the aisle to receive counsel. In fact, I didn't even wait for Dr. Graham to finish his message and give the invitation. While he was preaching, I simply opened my heart to Christ by faith, and I was saved.

Those circumstances were quite different from the circumstances surrounding the conversion of Saul of Tarsus, who became the apostle Paul. He was blinded by a bright light from heaven; he had a vision of the Lord Jesus in glory; and Jesus even spoke to him from heaven! Saul fell to the ground in fear and was blind for three days before God opened his eyes. None of those things happened to me, but I was born again just the same because I trusted Jesus Christ.

So, each conversion is amazing, but the circumstances of some conversions are more amazing than others. That includes the conversion of the thief on the cross. In spite of the fact that no startling miracles occurred, the conversion of the thief on the cross was one of the most marvelous spiritual experiences recorded in Scripture.

Here's the record from Luke's Gospel:

And the people stood looking on. But even the rulers with them sneered, saying, "He saved others; let Him save Himself if He is the Christ, the chosen of God." The soldiers also mocked Him, coming and offering Him sour wine, and saying, "If You are the King of the Jews, save Yourself." And an inscription also was written over Him in letters of Greek, Latin, and Hebrew: THIS IS THE KING OF THE JEWS. Then one of the criminals who were hanged blasphemed Him, saying, "If You are the Christ, save Yourself and us." But the other, answering, rebuked him, saying, "Do you not even fear God, seeing you are under the same condemnation? And we indeed justly, for we receive the due reward of our deeds; but this Man has done nothing wrong." Then he said to Jesus, "Lord, remember me when You come into Your kingdom." And Jesus said to him, "Assuredly, I say to you, today you will be with Me in Paradise." (Luke 23:35–43)

"Today you will be with Me in Paradise" was our Lord's second statement from the cross. The first statement was "Father, forgive them; for they do not know what they do" (Luke 23:34). Our Lord first prayed for his enemies, but in his second statement, he spoke to a repentant sinner and gave him assurance that he was going to heaven when he died. Consider the amazing aspects of this man's conversion.

The Amazing Situation

You can't help but be struck by the amazing situation at Calvary. When they crucified our Lord Jesus, they put him between two thieves. They could have put the two thieves together, which would have been the natural thing to do, for it appears that these two thieves were partners in crime and knew each other. Instead, the Roman soldiers put the Lord Jesus between the two thieves and created an amazing situation. What made it so amazing?

Prophecy Was Fulfilled

Jesus hanging between two thieves was the fulfillment of prophecy. Isaiah 53:12 tells us that "He was numbered with the transgressors." Mark wrote in his Gospel: "With Him they also crucified two robbers, one on His right and the other on His left. So the Scripture was fulfilled which says, 'And He was numbered with the transgressors'" (Mark 15:27–28).

At the "place of the skull" where Jesus was crucified, not only were the wicked hands of men at work, but also the powerful hands of God. Without realizing it, wicked men were obeying the plan of God and fulfilling divine prophecy (Acts 2:23). God's promise is, "I am watching to see that my word is fulfilled" (Jer. 1:12 NIV), and his Word will never fail.

Jesus was numbered with the transgressors because evil men had concluded that he was a transgressor. The sinless

Son of God was treated like a criminal! But we shouldn't be surprised at this, because it was for sinners that Jesus came into the world. "You shall call His name JESUS, for He will save His people from their sins" (Matt. 1:21). "Just as the Son of Man did not come to be served, but to serve, and to give His life a ransom for many" (Matt. 20:28). Jesus lived with sinners and was even derisively called "a glutton and a winebibber, a friend of tax collectors and sinners" (Matt. 11:19). He died with sinners, and he died for sinners.

God's Gracious Providence

But there was something else amazing about that situation on Golgotha: Jesus was crucified between two thieves because God was working out his gracious providence. The word "providence" means "to see to it beforehand." There were no accidents in the life of the Lord Jesus, only appointments. It was not accidental that the Lord Jesus was between these two thieves, because the Father was working out his gracious providential plan.

To begin with, because Jesus was between the two thieves, both thieves could hear his repeated prayer, "Father, forgive them, for they do not know what they do" (Luke 23:34). The Holy Spirit of God used that prayer to speak to the hearts of those two criminals, "Here is One Who forgives sinners and prays that God would be merciful to them."

Because those thieves were on either side of the Lord Jesus, they could both see the title that Pilate had put on the cross. When you combine the Gospel records, you learn that the complete title was: "This is Jesus of Nazareth, the King of the Jews." It was written in three languages, and the thieves probably knew at least two of those languages. We might say that Pilate wrote the first "gospel tract," and it hung over the head of the Lord Jesus.

No doubt those two thieves looked at each other as they spoke to one another, and this meant they had to look at the Lord Jesus hanging between them. As they looked at the Lord Jesus, they had to see that title, which told them who he was and what he was.

He is Jesus, which means "Savior." The name "Jesus" is from the Jewish name "Joshua" which means "Jehovah is Savior." Like the Old Testament Joshua, Jesus leads people into their inheritance, if they will trust him and call upon him; for "whoever calls upon the name of the LORD shall be saved" (Acts 2:21; Rom. 10:13).

He is "Jesus of Nazareth," which means he came from a despised and a rejected city (John 1:46) and was identified with the outcasts. He is "King of the Jews," which means he is a Savior who has a kingdom! So, in reading this title, they could learn the good news that this man called Jesus was not a criminal, though he was hanging on a cross. He was the Savior of lost sinners, the King of the Jews.

Consider a third fact: because of this amazing situation, both thieves could hear the crowd as it railed upon him. The soldiers mocked him: "If You are the king of the Jews, save Yourself" (Luke 23:37). The common people and the religious rulers of the nation mocked him and said, "He saved others; let Him save Himself if He is the Christ, the chosen of God" (Luke 23:35). That was certainly good news if only the thieves would believe it; if he saved others, he could save them!

Pilate put that superscription on the cross to quiet his own conscience, but God used it to win a lost soul. The soldiers and the rulers mocked the Lord Jesus, but God used their mockery to transform a criminal into a repentant sinner. How amazing is the working of the gracious providence of God!

Each of the thieves had access to the Lord Jesus. They didn't have to make special efforts to hear him or speak to him, because Jesus was right there between them. As the thieves called back and forth to each other, they looked at

Jesus. As they looked at him, they saw something different about him. He wasn't denouncing the soldiers the way other victims usually did, nor was he answering those who reviled him. No wonder the believing thief confessed, "This Man has done nothing wrong" (Luke 23:41). God still works providentially to create situations that give people opportunity to meet Christ, trust him, and be saved. No one is ever saved by accident, for meeting Jesus Christ is a divine appointment. God sets up the situation to give sinners the opportunity to hear the gospel, trust Jesus Christ, believe on him, and be saved. The Lord is "not willing that any should perish but that all should come to repentance" (2 Peter 3:9). God's desire is that all men be saved (1 Tim. 2:3–4). What a tragedy when people miss that golden opportunity to trust Jesus and be forgiven.

The Amazing Supplication

"Lord, remember me when you come into Your kingdom" (Luke 23:42). It isn't a long complicated prayer, but it is still one of the most amazing prayers recorded in the Bible. Why? Consider several reasons.

The Confession Contained in His Prayer

When he prayed that simple prayer, this dying thief admitted that he feared God. He was not an agnostic, questioning the existence of God, or an atheist, denying the existence of God. He didn't conceive of God as a far-off Creator whose ear was deaf to the cries of poor sinners. This man feared God, so he wanted to be ready to meet God when he died.

The hypocritical Jewish religious leaders standing with the crowd around the cross would have claimed that they feared God, but there was no evidence of fear either in their words or their actions. They were crucifying their own Messiah and mocking him as he suffered and died! "The fear of the LORD is the beginning of wisdom" (Ps. 111:10), but these pious men were acting in ignorance (Acts 3:17) and didn't realize what they were doing. "By the fear of the LORD one departs from evil" (Prov. 16:6), but these proud men were committing the greatest crime in human history by killing their own Messiah.

He confessed that he was guilty. The thief admitted that he and his companion had broken the law and were justly condemned. It's rare to find criminals who will admit they've done wrong and deserve to be punished. I think it was Frederick the Great who once visited a prison where he listened to prisoner after prisoner protest his innocence and ask the emperor to release him. But one man humbly confessed that he was guilty and deserved to be in prison.

"Release this man!" ordered the emperor. "It's unwise to have him here polluting all these innocent men!"

Sinners can't be saved until they first admit their guilt and that they deserve to be condemned and punished by the Lord: "that every mouth may be stopped, and all the world may become guilty before God" (Rom. 3:19). Before you can open your mouth and call on the Lord for salvation, your mouth must be shut in conviction.

The repentant thief confessed that Jesus Christ was innocent. But if he were innocent, why was he dying on a cross along with two guilty criminals? Why were the leading people of the city accusing and abusing him? The thief knew that Jesus was innocent because of the conviction in his own heart. Our Lord's words, his prayer, and his attitude toward his enemies all spoke of purity and love. This Jesus of Nazareth was different from other men, and the thief sensed the difference.

He confessed that there is life after death and that he was accountable to God. "Do you not even fear God?" he asked his friend, and then he added "for we receive the due reward of our deeds" (Luke 23:40–41). We live today in a "no-fault" world, whether you're in an auto accident, seeking a divorce, or trying to win a court case. Like Adam and Eve, we look for somebody to blame, but we don't want God to blame us.

The thief knew that he was dying and that after death he would meet God. He knew that his excuses wouldn't convince God that he was innocent. Quite to the contrary, he confessed that he was guilty and that he couldn't face eternity without a Savior. That's why he turned to Jesus.

Do you believe that there is indeed life after death? Are you prepared for it? Do you believe that you deserve judgment, that you are a guilty sinner? Do you believe that there is a just and holy God and that you will have to answer to him one day? Death is a divine appointment, and after death comes another divine appointment: the judgment (Heb. 9:27). Are you ready? The dying thief was ready because he put his faith in Jesus Christ.

The Courage It Took to Pray the Prayer

As far as the biblical record is concerned, nobody else on Calvary was asking Jesus for salvation. The priests and religious rulers were mocking Christ, and yet this thief dared to believe on Jesus and do it publicly. The crowd was opposing him, the solders were laughing at him, and the thief's own friend was mocking the Lord Jesus. In spite of all that pressure, the thief trusted Jesus. Some people don't want to trust the Lord Jesus because they're afraid of what other people might do or say; yet here was a man who had the courage to defy the rulers, the priests, the soldiers, and his own friend by turning to the Lord Jesus and trusting him.

Revelation 21:8 lists eight different classes of people who are not going to heaven, and the first class on the list is "the fearful" or "the cowardly." These are the people who don't have the courage to admit their need and turn to Christ for salvation. They have the courage to sin openly with their friends, but lack the courage to repent in spite of their friends. They're afraid of what people might say if they leave the crowd and take their stand for Christ. This thief wasn't among the cowardly. He courageously identified with Christ when almost everybody else was against him.

The Confidence This Prayer Demanded

Just think of how little this thief really understood about Jesus and the way of salvation. He could read the accusation posted above our Lord's head and certainly he heard the voices of the people around the cross. As we have seen, the name "Jesus" means "Savior," so the thief knew Jesus could save him. He also heard the mockers crying, "He saved others!" He could have reasoned, "If this Jesus saved others, he can also save me."

The notice on the cross said that Jesus was a king and therefore had a kingdom. If he had a kingdom, he had authority, and he could exercise that authority for others. Jesus came from Nazareth, a city disdained by the people of Judea. "Can anything good come out of Nazareth?" asked Nathanael (John 1:46). But the very title "Jesus of Nazareth" identified him with the common people, and that was the kind of Savior this thief needed.

Many people say, "I would like to be saved, but I want to understand more about it." Understanding the gospel is a part of salvation, but you don't have to become a theologian to become a Christian. This thief didn't understand a great deal about the things of God, but what he did understand led him to faith in the Savior. He's a witness against sinners today who know the truth of the gospel, who have heard Sunday school lessons and sermons about Jesus, who have even sung songs about Jesus, and yet have rejected him. Their judgment will be far greater than that of people who have never heard about the Savior.

Furthermore, this thief saw the Lord Jesus when he was rejected, abused, weak, and dying. Would you trust someone who was in that condition, hanging helpless on a cross? It's like expecting help from a drowning lifeguard! I could understand people trusting the Lord Jesus if they saw him do a miracle, but Jesus didn't do a miracle as he hung on the cross. Jesus was forsaken, mocked, and laughed at; yet this thief had the faith to trust him.

Today God invites you to trust a Savior who is risen and glorified, who is seated on the throne of the universe. There's no problem trusting that kind of a Savior! This thief didn't have a great deal of knowledge. He didn't see a beautiful sight as he looked at the Lord Jesus; yet this man believed on Jesus and was saved. His faith ranks among the greatest recorded in the Bible.

The Amazing Salvation

There's a third aspect to the thief's conversion that is amazing, not only the situation and the supplication, but also the salvation. When he trusted Jesus, he received far more than he expected! "But where sin abounded, grace abounded much more" (Rom. 5:20).

The thief knew that he was a lost sinner, but the Lord Jesus Christ came "to seek and to save that which was lost" (Luke 19:10). People who won't admit that they're lost cannot be saved. One of the problems we face as we share the gospel today is the unwillingness of people to admit their need to be saved. They think they have enough "good works" stored up to merit a home in heaven. They don't realize that they're lost sheep on the broad road that leads to destruction, instead of children of God on the narrow road that leads to life.

This thief was a lost man who knew he was lost. He was a condemned man who knew he was condemned. Because of this, he turned to the Lord Jesus and said, "Lord, remember me when You come into Your kingdom" (Luke 23:42). And Jesus gave to him an amazing salvation: "Assuredly, I say to you, today you will be with Me in Paradise" (v. 43). What are the characteristics of this salvation that make it so amazing?

Salvation Wholly by Grace

To begin with, this salvation was wholly by God's grace. The dying thief didn't deserve to be saved, which he admitted. He confessed that he and his friend were justly receiving "the due reward" for the crimes they had committed (Luke 23:40–41). He gave no excuses, he offered no alibis; he simply confessed that he was a sinner who deserved to die. Jesus heard the man's cry and saved him by his grace.

Grace is simply the undeserved favor of God. You can't earn it, buy it, or work for it. You can only receive grace as a gift.

But that demands honesty and humility: honesty in admitting that you need to be saved, and humility in confessing that you can't save yourself. Whenever somebody gives us a gift, we immediately feel obligated to do something in return in order to deserve the gift. But that approach won't work with God. Salvation is a gift—a free gift—and there are no strings attached.

The first man, Adam, became a thief when he and Eve took from the forbidden tree and disobeyed God (Gen. 3). Because Adam was a thief, he was cast out of Paradise. The last Adam, Jesus Christ, turned to a thief and said, "Today you will be with Me in Paradise." That is the grace of God! In his mercy, God doesn't give us what we do deserve; in his grace, God gives us what we don't deserve. What an amazing salvation!

This thief was in no position to earn his salvation. Some people claim that in order to go to heaven you must keep the Ten Commandments or obey the Sermon on the Mount. Now, obeying the Lord is an important thing, but nobody can be saved by obeying either the Ten Commandments or the Sermon on the Mount. The dying thief didn't have adequate time or moral strength to keep the Ten Commandments or the Sermon on the Mount. In a short time, he would meet his Maker and be judged. What he needed was grace, not law.

Others say that in order to get to heaven you have to go through some religious ritual. But the dying thief didn't have an opportunity to participate in a religious ritual. Let's not complicate God's free gift of salvation. This man's conversion was wholly because of the grace of God. The thief didn't deserve to be saved nor did he earn his salvation. He simply received the gift of salvation by faith.

Have you received salvation as a gracious gift from God? Or are you bragging about your religious activities, how much you pray, how many meetings you attend, how many good works you perform? If so, you may not be saved at all. When you're truly saved, it's wholly by the grace of God, and you don't brag about it. "For by grace you have been saved through faith, and that not of yourselves; it is the gift of God, not of works, lest anyone should boast" (Eph. 2:8–9).

But God's grace isn't cheap; it cost God's Son his life on the cross. He paid the price for us, and faith in him is the only way we can be forgiven and one day enter heaven to be with Jesus.

Salvation That Is Certain

There's something else about this amazing salvation: it was certain and secure. It wasn't a "hope-so" salvation, not a "guess-so" salvation. Listen again to the words of Jesus to this man: "Assuredly, I say to you, today you will be with Me in Paradise." How did this man know that his salvation was secure? Because Jesus told him so, and the Lord gives us the same assurance in his Word today. "Whoever calls on the name of the LORD shall be saved" (Acts 2:21). "He who has the Son has life; he who does not have the Son of God does not have life" (1 John 5:12). The Word of God can be trusted. "For ever, O LORD, thy word is settled in heaven" (Ps. 119:89 KJV).

Some people claim that you can't know if you're saved until you die, but that's not what Scripture teaches. I don't want to gamble on eternity; I want to know before I die that I'm going to heaven. Paul wrote, "For I know whom I have believed and am persuaded that He is able to keep what I have committed to Him until that Day" (2 Tim. 1:12). And John wrote, "These things I have written to you who believe in the name of the Son of God, that you may know that you have eternal life" (1 John 5:13).

The dying thief knew that he had eternal life and that he would be with Jesus in heaven. He was an undeserving sinner, a thief, a condemned criminal, and yet he knew he was going to heaven. How did he know it? Jesus told him so.

A Personal Salvation

The salvation Jesus gave to this man was personal. Jesus spoke to this man personally and saved him personally. "Assuredly, I say to you. . . ." (Luke 23:43). God loves us personally. Writing about Jesus Christ, Paul said " . . . who loved me and gave Himself for me" (Gal. 2:20). The Lord Jesus Christ died for us personally. God's love is shown to us personally, and God saves us personally. God doesn't deal with sinners as part of a crowd; he doesn't save people en masse. God saves people individually, one by one.

A Present Salvation

It was a personal salvation and it was a present salvation: "Today you will be with me in Paradise." Notice the word "today." The man had said, "Lord, remember me when You come into Your kingdom" (Luke 23:42), as though the thief were saying, "Sometime in the future, when you enter Your kingdom, please remember me." But you can paraphrase our Lord's reply: "Why wait until the future? I'm a King today! I'll give you salvation right now."

Salvation is not a process. You don't receive the forgiveness of sins on the installment plan. Salvation is an instantaneous spiritual experience by the power of God when you put your faith in Jesus Christ. To be sure, spiritual birth must be followed by spiritual growth (2 Peter 3:18), but the growth is the evidence of the birth, not the cause of it. One of the old hymns says it perfectly:

> 'Tis done, the great transaction's done!
> I am my Lord's and He is mine.
> (Philip Doddridge)

Salvation Centered in Christ

Salvation means being related by faith to Jesus Christ. Our Lord identified with this man in condemnation, and this man was identified with Jesus Christ in salvation. That's what the cross is all about. Salvation isn't centered in Moses or in keeping the Law. It's not centered in a preacher, a church, or a revered tradition. Salvation is centered in Jesus Christ.

This thief couldn't turn to the other thief and say, "Remember me when you come into your kingdom"; his friend didn't have a kingdom. Nor could the dying thief turn to one of the Roman soldiers and plead, "Remember me when you come into your kingdom"; the soldiers knew nothing of an eternal kingdom. The dying man couldn't turn to one of the religious leaders; they could do nothing for him. He could only turn to Jesus Christ. "Nor is there salvation in any other, for there is no other name under heaven given among men by which we must be saved" (Acts 4:12).

How often we hear the old argument, "Just as there are many roads to New York City, so there are many ways to heaven." But we aren't talking about going to an earthly city built by men; we're talking about a heavenly city built by God. Men can construct as many roads as they please to their cities, but God has declared there's only one way to his city: Jesus Christ, the Savior of the world. Jesus said, "I am the way, the truth, and the life. No one comes to the Father except through Me" (John 14:6).

Have you ever turned to Jesus Christ and asked him to save you? The salvation he gives is wholly by grace; it's certain and secure; it's personal; it can be yours right now. Salvation is centered in Jesus Christ, so all you have to do is turn to him, repent of your sins, and receive the gift by faith.

A Glorious Salvation

All the man had asked for was a share in some kind of a future kingdom about which he knew very little. But the Lord Jesus gave him far more than he ever expected: the believing thief would be with Jesus in paradise! Paradise is the third heaven, where God dwells (2 Cor. 12:1–4). Heaven is a real place, a glorious place, where there will be no pain, sorrow, tears, or death. Heaven is where Jesus is now, preparing a place for all who have trusted him. One day, he will return and take his people to heaven to dwell with him forever (John 14:1–6).

A man said to me one day, "I'm going to be like that dying thief. I'm going to wait until the very last minute, and then I'll trust Jesus as my Savior."

But this approach to salvation presents two great problems. First, you don't know when that "last minute" will come. Would you sign a paper right now saying, "I will postpone the salvation of my soul until just a few minutes before I die"? Of course not, because you don't know when your last minute will come.

But there's an even greater problem. The dying thief isn't an example of a sinner saved the last opportunity he had; he's an example of a sinner saved the first opportunity he had! We have no reason to believe that this man had heard Jesus preach before they met at Calvary. When he had his first opportunity, the thief trusted in Jesus Christ. That's what every lost sinner should do.

The only difference between this thief and lost sinners today is that he got caught, and they haven't been caught yet! One day, every lost sinner will receive the due reward for his or her deeds, and then it will be too late. Today you can meet Jesus as your Savior, but tomorrow you may meet him as your Judge.

Soon after this thief trusted Christ, the darkness came and shrouded the cross and the land. "Walk while you have the light, lest darkness overtake you," said Jesus. "While you have the light, believe in the light, that you may become sons of light" (John 12:35–36).

> The dying thief rejoiced to see
> That fountain in his day.
> And there may I, though vile as he,
> Wash all my sins away.

"Today you will be with Me in Paradise."

7

OUR LORD SPEAKS TO HIS OWN

I f you and I had been in Jerusalem when Jesus was crucified, how near to his cross would we have stood? It's one thing to stand in a comfortable church sanctuary and sing "Jesus, keep me near the cross," but quite something else to actually do it. After all, Jesus was "despised and rejected of men," and it would have taken a great deal of courage and love to stand by his cross.

The Roman soldiers were standing near the cross because they had to be there; it was their duty. Four women were there, because they all loved Jesus. They were there out of devotion, not duty. They wanted to be with Jesus. Mary, the mother of our Lord, was there, and so were Mary Magdalene and Salome, his mother's sister. Salome was also the wife of Zebedee and the mother of James and John. Mary, the wife of Cleophas, was standing there, and so was the beloved disciple John.

"When Jesus therefore saw his mother, and the disciple whom he loved standing by, He said to his mother, 'Woman, behold your son!' Then He said to the disciple, 'Behold your mother!' And from that hour that disciple took her to his own home" (John 19:26–27). That disciple, of course, was John, who wrote the Gospel of John where this record is found.

Christians today use the phrase "near the cross" to describe their dedication and devotion to Jesus. The phrase has almost become an evangelical cliche. Perhaps we've prayed, "Lord, keep me near the cross" but we haven't stopped to think what we're really praying and if we're willing to pay the price to have our prayer answered. The Lord may say to us as he said to James and John, "You do not know what you ask" (Matt. 20:22).

Obviously, being near the cross isn't a matter of physical geography. Our Lord's cross is gone and nobody is able to go outside the city of Jerusalem and stand near it the way John and the women did centuries ago. Today, being near the cross refers to a spiritual position, a special relationship to Jesus Christ. To be near the cross means to identify with Christ in his suffering and shame, to go "outside the camp, bearing His reproach" (Heb. 13:13). It's what Paul called "the fellowship of His sufferings" (Phil. 3:10).

The third statement our Lord made from the cross helps us to understand what it means to be near the cross. Perhaps the best way to approach our study would be to talk to some of the people who were there. Let's interview Mary Magdalene, Salome, the mother of our Lord, and the apostle John to discover what it really means to be near the cross of Jesus Christ.

Mary Magdalene: A Place of Redemption

Mary Magdalene is listed last in John 19:25, but I want to start with her. If you had walked up to Mary Magdalene that afternoon and asked, "Mary Magdalene, what does it mean to you to be standing near the cross of Jesus?" I think she would have answered, "To me, this is a place of redemption."

The Lord Jesus Christ had redeemed Mary Magdalene and set her free from the terrible bondage of demonism. According to Luke 8:2 and Mark 16:9, she had been delivered from seven demons. It's unfortunate that people have confused the woman described in Luke 7:36–50 with Mary Magdalene. We don't know this woman's name, but we do know her reputation. She was a prostitute whom Jesus had delivered from sin. To show her love and appreciation for Jesus, she came into the house where Jesus was dining and anointed him with expensive perfume. Bondage to Satan is a terrible thing, and Jesus can deliver us. He can turn sinners "from darkness to light, and from the power of Satan to God, that they may receive forgiveness of sins and an inheritance among those who are sanctified by faith" in Jesus Christ (Acts 26:18).

> He breaks the power of canceled sin,
> He sets the prisoner free;
> His blood can make the foulest clean,
> His blood availed for me.
> (Charles Wesley)

When you trust the Lord Jesus Christ, you go from darkness to light, and from the power of Satan to the power of God. God begins to control and to use your life. You go from guilt to forgiveness, and you go from poverty to wealth as an heir of God through faith in Jesus Christ. This is what Jesus did for Mary Magdalene.

This miracle of redemption is a costly thing. When Jesus delivered Mary Magdalene from the power of Satan, it cost him his life. "Now is the judgment of this world; now the ruler of this world will be cast out. And I, if I am lifted up from the earth, will draw all peoples to Myself" (John 12:31–32). Standing there at the cross, Mary watched Jesus pay the price of her redemption.

Jesus had to die that we might be set free. For us to move out of the darkness into the light, he had to move from the light into the darkness. For us to be delivered from Satan to God, Jesus Christ had to be handed over to wicked men and then forsaken by God. For us to be delivered from guilt to forgiveness, Jesus had to be made sin for us. For him to make me rich, he had to become the poorest of the poor.

No wonder Mary was standing at the cross! And that's not all. She was at the tomb when Jesus was buried, and she was at the tomb early on resurrection morning. Mary Magdalene had experienced redemption, and Jesus was precious to her. As she stood near the cross, Mary could sincerely say, "The cross to me is a place of redemption."

In your life, is the cross a place of redemption? If so, then you can say, "I've trusted Jesus Christ, and he has moved me from darkness to light, from the power of Satan to the power of God, from the guilt of sin to forgiveness, from poverty to an inheritance through faith in him." "He has delivered us from the power of darkness and translated us into the kingdom of the Son of His love" (Col. 1:13).

Salome: A Place of Rebuke

The second person we want to talk to is Salome. She was Mary's sister, the mother of James and John, and the wife of Zebedee. We remember her as the woman who came to Jesus with her sons, asking him to let them be enthroned on his right hand and his left hand in his kingdom (Matt. 20:20–28).

Jesus asked the two brothers, "Are you able to drink the cup that I am about to drink, and be baptized with the baptism that I am baptized with?" James and John were so self-confident, they replied, "We are able." Jesus said, "You will indeed drink My cup, and be baptized with the baptism that I am baptized with." James was the first of the apostles to be martyred (Acts 12:1–2), and John was the last of the apostles to die, but he experienced suffering and persecution before he was called home. If we had asked Salome what the cross meant to her, I think she would have replied, "The cross to me is a place of rebuke. I stand here rebuked because of my selfishness. I wanted my two sons to have the places of honor at the right hand and the left hand of the Lord Jesus. I stand here seeing Jesus on a cross, not a throne, and I'm ashamed of myself for praying as I did."

Indeed, she might well be ashamed of herself, as all of us should be ashamed when we pray selfishly. "You ask and do not receive, because you ask amiss, that you may spend it on your pleasures" (James 4:3). Salome wanted something grand and glorious for her sons, but she didn't consider what the answer to her prayer would cost them and her. Her prayer was born of pride, not of humility. She was concerned only about her sons, not about the glory of the Lord.

Thrones are something you have to deserve, and for Jesus, the way to the throne was through the cross. First the suffering, then the glory. Salome had forgotten the cost of reigning with Jesus: "If we suffer, we shall also reign with him" (2 Tim. 2:12 KJV). If we want to wear the crown, we must be willing to drink the cup.

> When I survey the wond'rous cross,
> On which the Prince of glory died,
> My richest gain I count but loss,
> And pour contempt on all my pride.
> Forbid it, Lord, that I should boast
> Save in the death of Christ my God;
> All the vain things that charm me most,
> I sacrifice them to His blood.
>
> (Isaac Watts)

No Christian rises any higher than his or her prayer life, and sometimes the selfish things we do come from selfish praying. Salome couldn't bring her request for thrones to the cross, because her prayer was selfish, proud, and ignorant. She didn't realize the price that must be paid to earn a throne. James did pay a price, for he laid down his life for Jesus. John also paid a price, exiled on the Isle of Patmos. Salome looked upon the cross as a place of rebuke, and she was right. How can we pray selfishly in the light of his suffering on the cross? How can we ask for easy lives when he had to endure so much? God delights to honor his servants, and one day we will share his eternal glory. But before the glory, there must first be suffering. "But may the God of all grace, who called us to His eternal glory by Christ Jesus, after you have suffered a while, perfect, establish, strengthen, and settle you" (1 Peter 5:10).

Mary Magdalene tells us that the cross is a place of redemption, and Salome tells us that the cross is a place of rebuke.

Now let's interview Mary, the mother of our Lord, to see what the cross meant to her.

Mary: A Place of Reward

If we had stood with Mary at Calvary and asked her what it meant to her to be near the cross, I think she would have replied, "The cross to me is a place of reward."

It's interesting to note that we find Mary at the beginning of the Gospel of John (chapter 2) and at the end of the Gospel of John (chapter 19), but not in the chapters between. In John 2, Mary attends a wedding and is involved in the joys of a feast. In John 19, she is involved in the sorrows of an execution and a burial. In John 2, the Lord Jesus displayed his power and glory as he turned water into wine. But in John 19, our Lord died in weakness and shame as he drank the cup of sorrow. He could have exercised his power and delivered himself, but had he done so he would not have completed the work of salvation. He did not come to save himself; he came to save us.

In John 2, we find Mary speaking to Jesus and suggesting that he help solve an embarrassing problem. In John 19, Mary is silent. Her silence, however, is very meaningful, for Mary was the one person whose testimony could have saved Jesus from the cross. The Jewish rulers knew that Mary was the mother of our Lord. All she had to do was say to the authorities, "I am his mother. I should know him better than anyone else. What he says about being the Son of God is not true; therefore, please set him free." The authorities would have jumped at the opportunity to prove that Jesus was a deceiver.

But Mary kept quiet! Do you know why she kept quiet? She could not lie about her Son whom she knew to be the very Son of God. As she stood by the cross, Mary's silence was testimony that Jesus Christ is the Son of God. If anybody knows a son, certainly it's his mother. If Jesus Christ were not what he claimed to be, Mary could have announced it and saved him. But she kept silent. To me, her silence is eloquent testimony that the Christ we worship is God the Son come in human flesh.

The cross was a place of reward for Mary. In what sense? In the sense that Jesus didn't ignore her but rewarded her by sharing his beloved disciple with her. Mary is to be honored, but she is not to be worshiped. We are told in the Gospel of Luke that Mary herself rejoiced in God her Savior (Luke 1:47). Mary was saved by faith like any other sinner. Elizabeth did not say to her, "Blessed are you above women." Elizabeth said, "Blessed are you among women" (Luke 1:42). Then Elizabeth added, "Blessed is she who believed" (Luke 1:45).

When Mary and Joseph brought the child Jesus into the temple, Simeon told Mary, "A sword shall pierce through your own soul also" (Luke 2:35). She felt that sword pierce her soul as she stood by the cross of Jesus.

Consider the pain that Mary experienced because she was chosen to be the mother of our Lord. When she was discovered with child, she began to suffer shame and reproach. Her pregnancy was misunderstood and the neighbors gossiped about her. She was married to Joseph, a poor carpenter. She gave birth to the Lord Jesus in a lowly stable. Then she and Joseph and Jesus had to flee from Bethlehem to Egypt to escape the sword of Herod, and yet innocent children died because of her son Jesus. I wonder how Mary felt when she heard that report. She rejoiced that her child was delivered, but she must have felt the sword in her own soul, knowing that innocent children had died.

When the Lord Jesus was a youth, he said to her and Joseph, "Did you not know that I must be about My Father's business?" (Luke 2:49). This began an experience of painful separation between Mary and her son. At times, Mary didn't understand him or what he was doing, and the sword pierced her own soul as she watched and listened. The psalmist said it so eloquently in Psalm 69:8: "I have become a stranger to my brothers, and an alien to my mother's children."

During Jesus' life, Mary suffered because of the way he lived and served; at the cross, she suffered because of the way he died. He died in public, crucified between two thieves, treated like a criminal. All kinds of people walked by and hurled abuse at him. It was such a cosmopolitan crowd that Pilate had to write his accusation in three different languages! Our Lord wasn't crucified in a hidden corner on a side street, but outside the city gate where the crowds moved in and out. He died publicly, on a day when thousands of visitors had come to Jerusalem to celebrate Passover. And Mary stood near the cross, feeling the sword go through her soul.

But Jesus saw her, and Jesus assured her of his love. He always does this. You may be experiencing a Calvary experience and suffering intensely because of something tragic that has happened to you. Remember, the Lord Jesus Christ always assures us of his love when our hearts are broken. He said to her, "Woman [a title of respect], behold your son!" (John 19:26). Was he speaking about himself? I don't think so; I think he was talking about John. Then he said to John, "Behold your mother!" (John 19:27).

When he spoke those brief sentences, what did Jesus accomplish? He established a new relationship between Mary and John. It was as though he said to Mary, "I'm returning to my Father in heaven. Because of this, you and I must have a whole new relationship. But in order to give peace to your heart, in order to heal your wounded heart, I'm giving you John as a beloved son." He assured her of his love as he took his choice disciple and made him Mary's adopted son. The Lord Jesus felt her sorrow, he knew her loneliness, and he rewarded her by giving to her the disciple whom he loved so dearly.

I read somewhere that the longest will ever probated was made up of four big volumes. There were 95,940 words in it! The shortest will on record was probated in Great Britain, and it has only three words to it: "All for mother."

Jesus had no valuable earthly possessions to give to anybody. The soldiers gambled for his clothes and that was all he had. What could he give to Mary? He gave John to Mary. From that very hour, John took her into his own house (John 19:27). To Mary, the cross was a place of reward, for God ultimately rewards those who have suffered because of him.

John: A Place of Responsibility

Now, we must speak to John.

"John, what does it mean to you to be near the cross?"

I think John would answer, "This is a place of responsibility. In receiving Mary into my home, I'm taking Jesus' place in caring for her."

Our Lord Jesus reigned from the cross. He was completely in control of himself and the situation. That's one reason why he refused to drink the stupefying wine before he was crucified, for he wanted to be in complete control of his faculties as he did the will of the Father.

By speaking these words, Jesus restored John. Remember, in the Garden John had forsaken him and fled along with the other disciples. The Shepherd had been smitten, and the sheep had scattered. But John came back to the cross and took his stand with Jesus. Now, John was restored and forgiven.

You and I may stray from God's path. We may disobey God's will. We may even deny our Lord as Peter did, but we can always come back and be forgiven. Calvary wasn't the safest place to stand or the easiest place to stand, but John came back and stood near the cross of Jesus. In my pastoral ministry, I've been with people as they've died, but I've never been in a situation like the one on Calvary. It took courage and love for John to come back, and the Lord Jesus received John and restored him. It was John who wrote, "If we confess our sins, He is faithful and just to forgive us our sins, and to cleanse us from all unrighteousness" (1 John 1:9).

Jesus not only restored John, but he also honored him. It was as though Jesus said, "John, you're taking my place. Be a son to Mary and care for her." But aren't all of God's people supposed to take his place now that he's gone back to heaven? Following his resurrection, Jesus said to his disciples, "As the Father has sent Me, I also send you" (John 20:21). You and I represent Jesus Christ in this world.

What does this mean? It means that if we claim to be Christians, we must live as Jesus lived when he ministered in this world, and we must faithfully represent him. "As He is, so are we in this world" (1 John 4:17). He is the light of the world (John 8:12) and we should be lights in the world (Matt. 5:14–16; Phil. 2:15). Our neighbors may not go to church or read the Bible, but they will watch our lives and read what we do and say. It's a tremendous responsibility to represent Jesus in this world, but by the power of the Spirit of God, we can be faithful witnesses (Acts 1:8). The cross is a place of responsibility. If we stay near the cross, we have the responsibility of loving the Lord Jesus and living for him in a world that has rejected him.

Near the cross is where Jesus wants us to be.

Near the cross is a place for lost sinners seeking salvation, because the cross is a place of redemption. If you have never trusted the Lord Jesus, you can be redeemed and transformed. Just come to the cross by faith and trust him. "Whoever calls on the name of the LORD shall be saved" (Acts 2:21).

Near the cross is a place of rebuke. Our pride and our selfishness fade away as we stand at the cross and see the Lord Jesus suffering for us.

Near the cross is a place of reward. No matter how many times your heart has been pierced and broken, God will reward you. He knows how to transform suffering into glory.

Near the cross is a place of responsibility. When we come to the cross, we identify with Jesus in the fellowship of his sufferings. Then we go to do the work he commissioned us to do as we take his place in this world.

Are you standing near the cross of Jesus?

THE CRY FROM THE DARKNESS

The first statement of our Lord from the cross shouldn't surprise us, because we expect Jesus to pray for his enemies (Luke 23:34). He taught forgiveness, and he came to bring forgiveness, so "Father, forgive them, for they do not know what they do" is what we expect to hear him say.

Nor are we surprised that he said to the dying thief, "Today you will be with Me in Paradise" (Luke 23:43). After all, Jesus came to earth to die so that those who trust him might one day be with him in heaven. "For Christ also suffered once for sins, the just for the unjust, that He might bring us to God" (1 Peter 3:18).

When Jesus spoke to Mary and the apostle John, his words don't surprise us because our Lord obeyed God's law. The fifth commandment instructs us to honor our father and our mother, and certainly Jesus did that both in his life and in his death. He not only bore our sins in his body (1 Peter 2:24), but he also bears our burdens and cares for us (1 Peter 5:7).

No, the first three statements from the cross don't surprise us. However, the fourth statement does, because it introduces an element of surprise and even of mystery. This is what the record says:

> Now from the sixth hour until the ninth hour there was darkness over all the land. And about the ninth hour Jesus cried with a loud voice, saying, "Eli, Eli, lama sabachthani?" that is, "My God, my God, why have You forsaken Me?" Some of those who stood there, when they heard that, said, "This Man is calling for Elijah!" Immediately one of them ran and took a sponge, filled it with sour wine, and put it on a reed, and offered it to Him to drink. The rest said, "Let Him alone; let us see if Elijah will come to save Him." (Matt. 27:45–49)

At least three mysteries are wrapped up in this third statement from the cross, and if we understand something of these mysteries, we can better understand what Jesus did for us on the cross.

A Great Mystery

Let's begin with the great mystery of the darkness around the cross. From noon until three o'clock in the afternoon, darkness was over all the land, a supernatural darkness that couldn't be explained. It wasn't caused by an eclipse (a most unlikely event during Passover season) or by a sandstorm. It was a supernatural darkness sent by the Father as his Son hung between heaven and earth. Why did he send this darkness? What kind of darkness was it?

The Darkness of Sympathy

The Creator was dying on the cross, and all creation, shrouded in darkness, was sympathizing with him. Isaac Watts had this in mind when he wrote:

Well might the sun in darkness hide,
And shut His glories in;
When Christ the mighty Maker died
For man the creature's sin.

When the first man and woman sinned, their disobedience affected all creation (Gen. 3:14–19). God could forgive their sin, but he couldn't spare them from the sad consequences of their sin, consequences that we experience even today. Instead of caring for a beautiful garden, Adam had to sweat for his daily bread. As he tilled the ground, he had to struggle with thorns and briars. The woman would experience pain and travail as she conceived and bore children. But worst of all, death came on the scene, for "the wages of sin is death" (Rom. 6:23) and "in Adam all die" (1 Cor. 15:22).

Everything in creation obeys God except man, and man has the most to lose by his disobedience. God tells the rain where to fall and the wind where to blow, and they obey him; God tells man what to do and what not to do, and man disobeys him. We have serious ecological problems today because of man's continued disobedience to God. Greed and selfishness have made men bad stewards of God's rich creation and have created problems that nations are struggling to solve.

Today, all creation is suffering because sin and death are reigning in this world (Rom. 5:14–21). "For we know that the whole creation groans and labors with birth pangs together until now" (Rom. 8:22). When Jesus died, he died to redeem creation, as well as to save lost humanity. In cruel mockery, some soldiers took thorns, made a crown, and put it on Christ's head; but in wearing that crown, Jesus announced that he was bearing creation's pain as well as man's sins. One day, creation shall be delivered from bondage and travail and the King shall reign in righteousness and glory. There will be no more disease, disasters, or death.

The Darkness of Solemnity

The darkness at the cross was also the darkness of solemnity. It was the most solemn moment in the history of the world as the Just One died for the unjust and the innocent Lamb of God shed his blood for guilty sinners. God sent three days of darkness to the land of Egypt before that first Passover, when the lambs were slain to protect the firstborn; and God sent three hours of darkness before the Lamb of God died for the sins of the world.

In those three hours of darkness, it's as though God were saying, "This is an hour of solemn judgment, far greater than the judgment I sent to Egypt." Speaking about his death, Jesus said, "Now is the judgment of this world; now the ruler of this world shall be cast out" (John 12:31). Our Lord's death on the cross was a solemn event because he bore the sins of the world and brought about the defeat of Satan, the prince of this world. In the Bible, one of the descriptions of hell is "outer darkness." Most people don't like to hear about hell; others, when they hear about hell, joke about it. But hell is no joke. Jesus spoke about "the outer darkness," a real place where sinners suffer the eternal consequences of rejecting Jesus Christ (Matt. 8:12; 22:13; 25:30).

Some careless people have the idea that hell is just "heaven with the lights turned out." They think that in hell they'll enjoy friendship and fellowship, just as they do with their sinner friends here on earth. "We don't care if we go to hell," they say glibly. "After all, we'll have plenty of company there!" But hell is a place of suffering, separation, and loneliness; it's not a place of friendship and fun. If hell isn't serious, why did Jesus die? If hell isn't real and terrible, then the cross of Christ is a mockery and his death a scandalous waste.

The Darkness of Secrecy

This supernatural darkness was the darkness of secrecy, as though God put a curtain around the cross. During those three hours, Jesus Christ accomplished the great work of redemption and died for the sins of the world.

The annual Day of Atonement was the only time in the year when the Jewish high priest was allowed to go into the Holy of Holies, and he had to go alone (Lev. 16). He brought with him the blood of the sacrifice and sprinkled it on the mercy seat and before the ark of the covenant. Only God saw him do it, because he ministered alone.

During those three hours of darkness, Jesus completed an eternal transaction with his Father and finished the work that he came to do (John 17:4). What was that work? The work of salvation, which he alone could accomplish. Jesus was silent for three hours, and then he spoke and said, "My God, My God, why have You forsaken me?" (Matt. 27:46). Jesus was sinless, yet he was made sin for us "that we might become the righteousness of God in Him" (2 Cor. 5:21).

A Greater Mystery

But a mystery even greater than the darkness around the cross is our Lord's loneliness on the cross. The Son of God was forsaken by his Father!

As you read the Gospel records of his final hours before Calvary, you see the Lord Jesus gradually moving into loneliness and rejection. He celebrated the Passover with his twelve apostles in the upper room, then Judas departed to betray him, and only eleven disciples remained. They went with him to the Garden of Gethsemane, and there he chose three—Peter, James, and John—to watch with him and pray. But they went to sleep!

When Jesus was arrested in the Garden, all the disciples forsook him and fled. Then two of the disciples, Peter and

John, followed the soldiers and went into the courtyard of the high priest's residence. There Peter denied the Lord three times. One disciple, John, went to the cross of Christ where he stood with the women, then Jesus sent him home to take care of Mary.

The men closest to Jesus forsook him, but at least the Father was with him. "And He who sent Me is with Me," said Jesus. "The Father has not left Me alone" (John 8:29). Jesus told his disciples, "Indeed, the hour is coming, yes, has now come, that you will be scattered, each to his own, and will leave Me alone. And yet I am not alone, because the Father is with Me" (John 16:32). But at the cross even the Father left him! What a profound mystery, the loneliness of the Savior on the cross!

Why was he forsaken of the Father? There may be many reasons, but certainly the greatest is that Jesus was made sin for us on the cross and God is too holy to look upon sin. Sin isolates us from ourselves and creates an emptiness within. Sin separates us from God and even from one another. When Adam and Eve sinned, they hid themselves from the Lord because they were guilty and afraid to face a holy God. Sinners have been running away ever since. Evangelist Billy Sunday said that sinners can't find God for the same reason criminals can't find a policeman: they aren't looking!

God has never forsaken anyone but his Son. You may have felt abandoned by God, but God has never forsaken you. If God forsook you for one second, you would die; "For in Him we live and move and have our being" (Acts 17:28). God was with Joseph in his trials in Egypt; he was with Daniel during his captivity in Babylon; he was with David during his exile in the wilderness of Judea; but he forsook his own Son when he was made sin for us on the cross.

Jesus was forsaken by the Father that we might never be forsaken. He went through darkness that we might have light. He experienced terrible isolation and loneliness that we might never be left alone. Hell is eternal loneliness, eternal isolation, "away from the presence of the Lord and from the glory of His power" (2 Thess. 1:9 NASB). On the day of judgment, Jesus will say to those who have rejected his grace, "I never knew you; depart from Me, you who practice lawlessness" (Matt. 7:23). "Depart from Me, you cursed, into the everlasting fire prepared for the devil and his angels" (Matt. 25:41).

The Scriptures don't describe what Jesus experienced during those three hours of darkness, but his experience climaxed in the cry, "My God, My God, why have You forsaken Me?" No lost sinner in hell can ever ask that question, because they know why they are there: they refused to receive the gift of eternal life through faith in Jesus Christ. "How often I wanted to gather your children together, as a hen gathers her chicks under her wings, but you were not willing!" (Matt. 23:37).

The Greatest Mystery

To me, the greatest mystery of all is the blindness of the people around the cross. They simply couldn't see who Jesus was and what he was doing for them.

Someone has said that our Lord's cross wasn't placed in a quiet sanctuary between two candles, but on a noisy thoroughfare between two thieves. He was crucified during the Feast of Passover, when the city of Jerusalem was crowded with people from many nations, Jewish pilgrims who had come to celebrate the feast. Roman soldiers were at the cross, and so were Jewish religious leaders who hurled insults at the Son of God. Yet, as far as we know, nobody in that crowd realized what was really taking place. They were in the dark.

Blind to the Scriptures

To begin with, they were blind to the Scriptures. Surely one of the priests or experts in the Jewish Law would have recognized that our Lord's cry was a quotation of Psalm 22:1, "My God, My God, why have You forsaken Me?" David first said it when he was surrounded by his enemies and felt abandoned. Yet, led by the Holy Spirit, David wrote in that psalm an extraordinary description of crucifixion; but crucifixion was not an Old Testament Jewish form of execution! There's no record that David ever saw anybody hanging on a cross. How, then, could he describe it so accurately?

Being a prophet (Acts 2:29–30), David was inspired by the Holy Spirit to write about the sufferings of our Lord on the cross. David described the darkness and light at Calvary (v. 2); the mockery of the unbelieving crowd (vv. 6–8); the physical suffering of the Savior, including the piercing of his hands and feet (vv. 14–16); the humiliation and shame he endured (v. 17); the gambling for his garments (v. 18); and the seeming hopelessness of the situation (vv. 19–21).[1]

Trained in the Old Testament Scriptures, the Jewish religious leaders who heard our Lord's cry should have recognized where it came from, but they were blind to their own Scriptures. Had they read Psalm 22, they surely would have been amazed at the parallels between David's words and what was happening to Jesus of Nazareth on the hill called Calvary. Had they further investigated the great messianic passages in the Old Testament, especially Isaiah 53 and Zechariah 9:9–10 and 12:10, they would have discovered that they were crucifying their own Messiah.

Blind to the Savior

Not only were they blind to the Scriptures, but they were blind to the Savior. Prophecy was being fulfilled before their very eyes, and yet the people couldn't see it! They thought Jesus was calling for the prophet Elijah, a man the Jewish people held in highest esteem and for whom they waited. They expected Elijah to return and prepare the way for the coming of Messiah, not realizing that John the Baptist had performed that ministry for Jesus (Matt. 17:10–13; John 1:19–21).

But Jesus wasn't calling for Elijah; he was quoting Psalm 22:1. If these people had not been blind to the Scriptures, they would have recognized Psalm 22:1; then they would have recognized their Savior. How tragic it is when people misunderstand the Word of God and draw the wrong conclusions! How skillful Satan is in blinding the minds of lost sinners so they will not see the glory of Jesus Christ (2 Cor. 4:3–6)!

Why were they blind to the very Son of God? Because they refused to abandon their theological prejudices and see Jesus of Nazareth as the Son of God, the Messiah sent from God. By seeing in their Scriptures only a glorious King, and not a suffering Savior, their scholars had "taken away the key of knowledge" and blinded the people to the truth. Jesus Christ is the key to understanding the Old Testament types and prophecies (Luke 24:44–48), and when you reject him, you have no "key" and no "light." If they had been willing to do his will, their eyes would have been opened to the truth (John 5:39; 7:17), but they would not obey God's will (Matt. 21:28–32).

Blind to Their Own Sin

They were blind to the Scriptures, blind to the Savior, and blind to their own sin. "But you denied the Holy One and the Just," Peter told the Jewish leaders, "and asked for a murderer to be granted to you, and killed the Prince of life, whom God raised from the dead, of which we are witnesses. . . . Yet now, brethren, I know that you did it in ignorance, as did also your rulers" (Acts 3:14–15, 17).

"Let's see if Elijah will come and take him down!" they said. But Jesus wasn't planning to come down from the cross. Though from another context, the words of Nehemiah make a splendid reply to the words of the crowd: "I am doing a great work, so that I cannot come down" (Neh. 6:3).

Nothing blinds the eyes of the heart like deliberately rejecting the witness that God gives to us by his works and his words. "But although He had done so many signs before them, they did not believe in Him" (John 12:37). That's why Jesus warned the people of his day, "While you have the light, believe in the light, that you may become sons of light" (John 12:36).

What a paradox is the cross of Christ! He went through darkness that we might have light. He was forsaken that we might be accepted. He was misunderstood that we might know the truth and be set free. He died that we might live.

But our Lord didn't remain in the darkness. When the three hours were ended, he gave a shout of victory—"It is finished!"—and willingly yielded up his spirit to the Father. He laid down his life for the sheep.

When the short story writer O. Henry was dying, he said, "Turn up the lights. I don't want to go home in the dark." No one who trusts Jesus Christ as Savior and Lord ever goes home in the dark, for "the path of the just is like the shining sun, that shines ever brighter unto the perfect day" (Prov. 4:18).

The cry from the darkness tells us how much Jesus had to suffer so that we might live forever in the light.

"I Thirst"

As we listen to the Lord Jesus speak from Calvary, the words we hear convince us that he loves us. This love is revealed in a special way in his fifth statement:

> After this, Jesus, knowing that all things were now accomplished, that the Scripture might be fulfilled, said, "I thirst!" Now a vessel full of sour wine was sitting there; and they filled a sponge with sour wine, put it on hyssop, and put it to His mouth. So when Jesus had received the sour wine, He said, "It is finished!" And bowing His head, He gave up His spirit. (John 19:28–30)

Our Lord was crucified at nine o'clock in the morning and spent the first three hours on the cross in broad daylight. Then the darkness came, and at the end of that darkness, he cried, "My God, my God, why have You forsaken me?" (Matt. 27:46). His first three statements centered on others—his enemies, the thief, and John and Mary. The central statement focused on the Father. But in the last three statements, our Lord focused on himself: his body—"I thirst"; his soul—"It is finished" (see Isa. 53:10); and his spirit—"Father, into Your hands I commit My spirit" (Luke

23:46). Body, soul, and spirit were all offered by the Lord Jesus Christ in total submission to his Father's will.

The shortest of all the statements that our Lord made from the cross is the one found in John 19:28: "I thirst!" In the Greek text, it's only one word of four letters, and it's the only statement from the cross in which our Lord referred to his own physical needs. This simple word reveals to us the heart of the Lord Jesus and enables us to see his love in a deeper way.

The simple statement "I thirst" helps us to see three portraits of Christ: the suffering Son of man, the obedient Servant of God, and the loving Savior of sinners.

The Suffering Son of Man

Jesus Christ was truly man. To deny his humanity is to rob yourself of a Savior who had a real body and entered into genuine human experiences—birth, growth, hunger, thirst, weariness, pain, and death. Liberal theologians have denied our Lord's deity, but in the early church there were those who questioned his humanity. These false teachers said that Jesus wasn't really a man but only appeared to be a man. This is one reason why John wrote his first epistle, to reaffirm the fact that Jesus Christ was truly man as well as truly God (1 John 1:1–3; 4:1–3).

Jesus was born as a baby. He grew up as a child and a youth. Our Lord was "holy, harmless, undefiled" (Heb. 7:26), the perfect God-man who never sinned, but he shared in the sinless infirmities of human nature. He ate and drank. He became weary and slept. He felt pain. He wept. He suffered. He died. All these experiences belong to our common humanity, and Jesus tasted each one of them.

When our Lord Jesus was on the cross, he felt the depths of both physical and spiritual suffering. When he came to Calvary, he was offered the same narcotic that the two thieves were offered. Apparently they partook of it, but he did not. He refused to drink the wine that was mingled with myrrh because he didn't want his senses to be stupefied in any way. When he died on the cross, our Lord was in perfect control of his faculties.

Whenever the Jewish high priest ministered in the sanctuary of God, he was warned not to drink strong drink (Lev. 10:8–11). So, when Jesus offered himself as the final sacrifice for sin on the cross, he didn't take strong drink. Again, he was in full control of himself and felt every pain associated with crucifixion and death. He was the suffering Son of man.

Do you know what this means for us today? It means that Jesus Christ is able to sympathize with us, to identify with our pains and our needs. I am not suggesting that it's wrong for us today to accept anesthesia when undergoing medical treatment. After all, when God performed the first "surgery" in the Garden of Eden, he put Adam to sleep! But I am suggesting that our Lord Jesus Christ, to become our merciful High Priest, endured great suffering in life and in death that he might better minister to us today.

Because of this, we can come boldly to the throne of grace, knowing that he understands us and can help us (see Heb. 4:16). We come to one who has felt our pain and sorrow and knows just how we feel. He knows the burdens we carry and the pain we endure, and he can give us the grace we need to keep on going.

Wherever you go, you find hurting people. The Scottish pastor John Watson used to say, "Be kind, for everyone you meet is fighting a battle." Many are experiencing physical pain, while others are suffering emotional pain that may not be as evident. The closer you get to people, the more you discover the burdens they carry and the battles they fight. When Jesus, the suffering Son of man, cried, "I thirst," he announced that he identified with our every need.

That truth encourages me to pray and trust him for the grace I need to keep going and not to quit. It encourages me to pray for others who hurt, knowing that they can also come to the throne of grace and find help in the time of need (Heb. 4:14–16). Our Lord experienced suffering and pain so that he might become our sympathetic High Priest and identify with us in the struggles of life.

The Obedient Servant of God

We aren't surprised that the Lord Jesus thirsted, because crucifixion is an agonizing form of death that creates intense thirst. As the victim hangs on the cross, exposed to the sun, his life juices are drained right out of him. Psalm 69 describes how Jesus felt hanging on the cross. "I am weary with my crying; my throat is dry; my eyes fail while I wait for my God" (v. 3). You can read Psalm 69 and discover a portrait of our suffering Savior, the obedient servant of God.

Why did Jesus say, "I thirst"? According to John 19:28, it was so that "the Scripture might be fulfilled." What Scripture? Psalm 69:21: "They also gave me gall for my food, and for my thirst they gave me vinegar to drink." Our Lord's great concern was not his own physical need so much as the need to obey the Word of God. In everything he said and did, Jesus obeyed the Word of God. He said, "My food is to do the will of Him who sent Me, and to finish His work" (John 4:34). More than twenty times in the four Gospels you find phrases like "that it might be fulfilled" or "then was fulfilled," because Jesus is the obedient Servant of God. He always did the Father's will.

Why was Jesus born in Bethlehem rather than in Jerusalem or Nazareth? Because the prophet Micah prophesied that Messiah would be born in Bethlehem (Micah 5:2). Why did Mary and Joseph take Jesus and go down to Egypt? Because the prophet Hosea said it would happen

(Hosea 11:1; Matt. 2:15). Why did Jesus minister in Galilee? In obedience to Isaiah 9:1–2 (see Matt. 4:12–17). During all of his life and ministry, Jesus obeyed the Word of God; in fact, he was "obedient to the point of death, even the death of the cross" (Phil. 2:8).

The most important thing in the life of God's children is to know the will of God and do it, no matter the cost. We should be obedient servants "doing the will of God from the heart" (Eph. 6:6). As Jesus got his directions from the Father through the Scriptures, so must we. This doesn't mean that the Bible is some kind of "magic book" that you can open at random and discover the will of God. That practice is superstition, not faith. But as we read the Word, meditate on it, and seek to obey what God says, we discover that the Spirit helps us make wise decisions and live in the will of God. Proverbs 3:5–6 is a promise that never fails.

When you and I hear the Lord Jesus say, "I thirst," it reminds us that we, too, must be obedient to the Word of God.

The Loving Savior of Sinners

We have seen two portraits of the Lord Jesus in this statement: the suffering Son of man and the obedient Servant of God. Now look at the third portrait: the loving Savior of sinners.

Jesus was thirsty, to be sure, because of the physical agony he was experiencing. But he had just come through those three hours of darkness when the sun had veiled its face, and in that time of darkness, he had cried, "My God, My God, why have You forsaken me?" (Matt. 27:46). That's when the Lord Jesus was made sin for us. When he completed that great transaction for our salvation, he endured our hell for us and was thirsty.

Hell is a place of thirst. In Luke 16, our Lord told about a man who died and woke up in the place of judgment, and in that place of judgment, he was thirsty. He begged for somebody to come and give him even a drop of water to soothe his pain. When my Lord died for me on the cross, when he entered the darkness of hell for me, he thirsted. Hell is a place of eternal thirst, where people will thirst endlessly and will never be satisfied. Please notice that there were several cups at Calvary. There was the cup of charity, when they offered Jesus the wine mingled with myrrh, an opiate to deaden his pain. That cup he rejected (see Mark 15:23). There was the cup of mockery when the soldiers at the cross ridiculed him and offered him wine (see Luke 23:36). There was the cup of sympathy when somebody put some sour wine on a sponge and lifted it to his dry lips (see John 19:29). But the most bitter cup of all was the cup of iniquity. He said in the Garden, "Shall I not drink the cup which My Father has given me?" (John 18:11). He drank to the full the cup of suffering that rightfully belonged to us.

In John 2, our Lord turned water into wine. In John 4, Jesus said to the Samaritan woman at the well of Sychar, "Whoever drinks of this water will thirst again, but whoever drinks of the water that I shall give him will never thirst" (John 4:13–14). This woman was trying to find satisfaction in sin, but sin never quenches our inner thirst; it only increases the desire but decreases the enjoyment.

In John 7, at the Feast of Tabernacles, our Lord cried out, "If anyone thirsts, let him come to Me and drink" (John 7:37). He was referring to that event in the life of Moses when he smote the rock and the water flowed out (see Exod. 17:6). Jesus was smitten on the cross for us that we might have the water of life that satisfies thirst forever.

There is no thirst in heaven. "They shall neither hunger anymore nor thirst anymore" (Rev. 7:16). The last invitation in the Bible reads:

And the Spirit and the bride say, "Come!" And let him who hears say, "Come!" And let him who thirsts come. Whoever desires, let him take the water of life freely. (Rev. 22:17)

The question today is not, "Do you thirst?" because all mankind has a thirst for reality, a thirst for God, a thirst for forgiveness, whether they realize it or not. The real question is "How long will you continue to thirst?" When you trust Jesus Christ as your Savior, you will never thirst again. If you reject him, you will thirst forever.

The Lord Jesus Christ thirsted on the cross that we might never thirst again. He is the suffering Son of man, he is the obedient Servant of God, he is the loving Savior of sinners. When you put your faith and trust in him, he will satisfy you, and you will never thirst again.

"It Is Finished!"

People today don't like to face the horror of the cross, so we embellish the cross and almost beautify it. We make the cross into a piece of lovely jewelry or a decoration in a church sanctuary or perhaps in a cemetery. But we must remember that, for its unfortunate victims, crucifixion meant shame, torture, and a slow agonizing death. Yet our Lord Jesus was "obedient to the point of death, even the death of the cross" (Phil. 2:8).

The sixth word from the cross is recorded in John 19:30: "So when Jesus had received the sour wine, He said, 'It is finished!' And bowing His head, He gave up His spirit." When you compare the Gospel records, you discover that he shouted this statement and with a loud voice cried out, "It is finished!" The sixth statement from the cross wasn't the whimper of a defeated man; it was the triumphant shout of victory of the Son of God, our Savior. At the age of thirty-three, most people are saying, "It is beginning." But at the age of thirty-three, Jesus was saying, "It is finished!" He didn't say, "I am finished." It wasn't the lament of a victim overwhelmed by his circumstances; it was the shout of a victor overcoming all his enemies. In the Greek language in which John wrote his Gospel, this statement was only one word of ten letters—*tetelestai*. In the Greek, it means, "It is finished, it stands finished, and it always will be finished."

I confess that I've started many projects that I've never finished. In my files are book manuscripts that have never been completed and sermon sketches that have never been developed into messages. However, I have a feeling that if the world never reads these books or hears these sermons, nothing will be lost. But if Jesus had not completed his Father's assignments, the whole world would have remained lost! At the close of his ministry, our Lord Jesus Christ was able to shout, "It is finished!" He left nothing undone that the Father had given him to do. "I have glorified You on the earth," he said. "I have finished the work which You have given Me to do" (John 17:4). Because of this, you and I have the assurance of eternal salvation.

Consider with me three important facts about this word that our Lord uttered: "Tetelestai—It is finished!"

"Tetelestai"—A Familiar Word

Though this word isn't recognized by most people in our contemporary world, it was a familiar word when our Lord was ministering on earth. Archaeologists have discovered many ancient Greek documents that help us better understand Bible words, because the New Testament was written in the common language of the Greek-speaking people of that day. When he inspired the New Testament, the Holy Spirit guided the writers to use marketplace words that were on the lips of people as they worked and played in Jesus' day. If you were to consult the New Testament Greek lexicons, you would learn that common people in Jesus' day used the word "tetelestai" in their everyday lives. Let's meet some of them.[1]

Servants

Servants and slaves used this word whenever they finished an assignment and reported that fact to their master. The servant would say, "Tetelestai—I have finished the work that you gave me to do." This meant that the task assigned was completed the way the master wanted it done and when he wanted it done.

Jesus Christ is God's holy servant (Phil. 2:5–11). The prophet Isaiah described him as God's suffering servant (Isa. 42:1–4; 49:1–6; 50:4–9; 52:13–53:12). Jesus Christ came to this earth as a servant because he had a special work to do. "I have finished the work which You have given Me to do" (John 17:4). When his disciples were arguing over which of them was the greatest, Jesus rebuked their selfishness by saying, "Yet I am among you as the One who serves" (Luke 22:27). He even took the place of a servant and washed their feet (John 13:1–17), but his greatest act of service was when he died for them and for us on the cross.

One day, all of us will have to give the Lord an account of our service. "So then each of us shall give account of himself to God" (Rom. 14:12). I sincerely trust that I'll be able to say what Jesus said, "I have glorified You on the earth. I have finished the work which You have given me to do" (John 17:4). Find the work God wants you to do and do it. You aren't alone, "for it is God who works in you both to will and to do for His good pleasure" (Phil. 2:13). Then one day in glory you'll be able to say as Jesus said, "I have finished the work which You have given Me to do."

Priests

The Greek priests also used this word. Whenever worshipers brought sacrifices to the temple dedicated to whatever god or goddess they worshiped, the priests had to examine the animal to make sure it was faultless. If the sacrifice was acceptable, the priest would say, "Tetelestai—it is perfect." The Jewish priests followed a similar procedure at the temple and used the equivalent Hebrew or Aramaic word. It was important that the sacrifice be faultless.

Jesus Christ is God's perfect, faultless sacrifice, the Lamb of God who died to take away the sin of the world (John 1:29). How do we know Christ is a faultless sacrifice? God the Father said so! When the Lord Jesus was baptized, the Father spoke from heaven and said, "This is My beloved Son, in whom I am well pleased" (Matt. 3:17). With those words, God the Father put his seal of approval upon God the Son. Then God the Holy Spirit came down as a dove and rested on Jesus, thus adding his witness to that of the Father (Matt. 3:16). Some of the religious leaders called Jesus a glutton and a winebibber (Matt. 11:19), but even the demons admitted that Jesus was the Son of God (see Matt. 8:28–29). His enemies had to admit that he was faultless, because they had to hire liars to bear false witness against him at his trial. Our Lord's followers, who lived in intimacy with him, found no fault in him. None of the apostles ever said, "We heard Jesus tell a lie" or "We saw Jesus commit a sin." Jesus is the perfect Savior, the Lamb of God "without blemish and without spot" (1 Peter 1:19).

Pilate, the Roman governor, admitted, "I find no fault in this Man" (Luke 23:4). Even Judas the traitor confessed, "I have sinned by betraying innocent blood" (Matt. 27:4). Yes, all who knew Jesus could say, "Tetelestai! He is the perfect, faultless sacrifice." There is no other sacrifice for sin that qualifies. Only Jesus Christ is perfect, spotless, and faultless.

Artists

The servants and priests used this word, but so did the artists. When artists completed their work, they would step back, look at it, and say, "Tetelestai—it is finished!" That meant, "The picture is completed."

If you ignore Jesus Christ, the Old Testament presents a rather dark picture that's difficult to understand. In the Old Testament you find ceremonies, prophecies, and symbols that don't seem to fit together into a logical pattern. The Old Testament is a book of many unfulfilled prophecies and unexplained ceremonies, and you don't get the "key" until you know Jesus Christ. Unless you know Jesus Christ, your reading of the Old Testament is like walking through a picture gallery with the lights dimmed. When Jesus Christ came, he completed the picture and turned on the lights! In his life, death, resurrection, and ascension, Jesus fulfilled the types and prophecies and explained the meaning of the "picture."

The Easter evening scene described in Luke 24 illustrates this truth. Two discouraged men are walking on the road to Emmaus, discussing Christ's death and trying to figure out what it meant. A stranger joins them, and they tell him about their dashed hopes and confused minds. (Can you imagine telling Jesus about his own death?) Jesus said to them, "O foolish ones, and slow of heart to believe in all that the prophets have spoken!" (Luke 24:25). Then, beginning at Moses and all the prophets, the Lord Jesus went through the Old Testament Scriptures and explained the total picture. He turned on the lights. His work on Calvary had completed the picture so that God's great plan of salvation was now clear to see. Because we know Jesus Christ, believers today can read the Old Testament and see the wonderful picture, even though there are still difficulties and things hard to understand. But the light is shining and the portraits are no longer in the shadows. Because of our Lord's finished work on the cross, we can see the complete picture that God has painted.

Merchants

"Tetelestai" was a word used by slaves, priests, and artists, but the merchants also used it. To them, the word meant "the debt is fully paid." If you had purchased something "on time," when you made the last payment the merchant would give you a receipt that read "tetelestai." It meant, "It is finished. The debt has been fully paid."

Unbelieving sinners are in debt to God and can't pay their bill. Having broken God's law, they are bankrupt and unable to pay (see Luke 7:36–50). But Jesus paid the debt when he died for us on the cross. That's what tetelestai means: the debt has been paid, it stands paid, and it always will be paid. When we turn to Christ in faith, our sins are forgiven and the debt is canceled forever.

"Tetelestai"—Spoken by a Faithful Savior

"Tetelestai" was a familiar word shouted by a faithful Savior. He came to do the Father's will and he did it. He came to purchase our redemption and he did it. He came to do a great work, the work of salvation, and he finished that work. From the beginning of his life on earth to the day he returned to the Father, Jesus was faithful to do what the Father commanded. "I delight to do Your will, O My God, and Your law is within My heart" (Ps. 40:8; see Heb. 10:1–18). He was faithful throughout his entire earthly life. When he was twelve years old, Jesus said, "Did you not know that I must be about My Father's business?" (Luke 2:49). At the wedding in Cana, where he performed his first miracle, Jesus said, "My hour has not yet come" (John 2:4). He knew he was on a divine timetable that would ultimately take him to the cross. He told his disciples, "My food is to do the will of Him who sent Me, and to finish His work" (John 4:34). On the Mount of Transfiguration, our Lord discussed with Moses and Elijah his "decease which He was about to accomplish at Jerusalem" (Luke 9:31). One day he said to his disciples, "I have a baptism to be baptized with, and how distressed I am till it is accomplished" (Luke 12:50). In his High Priestly prayer, he said, "I have glorified You on the earth. I have finished the work which You have given Me to do" (John 17:4). He could shout the word "tetelestai" because he was a faithful Savior who accomplished the Father's will. Jesus was faithful in spite of satanic opposition, in spite of the blindness and disobedience of the religious leaders, even in spite of the stupidity and slowness to believe of his own disciples. When sinful people were doing their worst, Jesus Christ was giving his best; and he did it because he loved the Father and loved a world of lost sinners. Jesus Christ is still a faithful Servant. Having finished His work on earth, he is now faithfully serving his people in heaven as High Priest and Advocate (Heb. 4:14–16; 1 John 2:1–3). When we're tempted, we can come to his throne and receive the grace and mercy we need. If we sin, we can come to our heavenly Advocate, confess our sins, and be forgiven (1 John 1:9–2:2). He is faithful to deliver us in times of temptation (1 Cor. 10:13), faithful to forgive us when we fall, and faithful to keep us until we meet him face to face (2 Tim. 1:12; Jude 24).

"Tetelestai"—A Finished Work

That leads us to the third fact. "Tetelestai" was a familiar word spoken by a faithful Savior about a finished work. When he shouted the word, it meant that all the Old Testament prophecies referring to his work on the cross were now fulfilled and finished. Beginning in Genesis 3:15, God had promised that a Savior would defeat Satan. All the pictures of Christ in the tabernacle furnishings, the priestly ministry, and the sacrificial system were completely finished and fulfilled. The Old Testament types and prophecies were fulfilled. The veil of the temple was torn in two, and man was able to enter into the presence of God. The way of salvation had been opened!

"It is finished" also means that the Old Covenant Law is finished. Some people are afraid of this truth, but it is as biblical as the virgin birth or the resurrection of Jesus. Colossians 2:14 says "having wiped out the handwriting of requirements that was against us, which was contrary to us. And He has taken it out of the way, having nailed it to the cross." We no longer live under the bondage of law; instead, we live in the freedom of God's grace (Rom. 6:15). The great word of the gospel isn't "do"; it's "done." The work of redemption has been finished!

Some years ago there was an eccentric evangelist whose name was Alexander Wooton. A man came to him one day and said rather flippantly, "What must I do to be saved?" Knowing the man wasn't serious about salvation, Wooton replied, "It's too late! You can't do anything!" The man became alarmed and said, "No, no! What must I do to be saved?" And Wooton replied again, "It's too late! It's already been done!" That's the message of the gospel: the work of salvation is completed. It is finished. There's nothing we can add to it, and to add to it would mean taking away from it. God offers the lost world a finished work, a completed salvation. All the sinner has to do is believe on Jesus Christ.

The Book of Hebrews explains this completed salvation: "But now, once at the end of the ages, He has appeared to put away sin by the sacrifice of Himself. And as it is appointed for men to die once, but after this the judgment, so Christ was offered once to bear the sins of many" (Heb. 9:26–28). "For it is not possible that the blood of bulls and goats could take away sins. . . . But this Man, after He had offered one sacrifice for sins forever, sat down at the right hand of God. . . ." (Heb. 10:4, 12). The work of salvation is completed. "It is finished!" Our Lord died, was buried, arose from the dead, and returned to glory. There he sat down because the work was finished (Heb. 1:3). In the Old Testament tabernacle, there were no chairs because the priests' work was never finished. But Jesus Christ sat down in heaven because his work was finished.

Since salvation is a finished work, we dare not add anything to it, take anything from it, or substitute anything for it. There is only one way of salvation: personal faith in the finished work of the Lord Jesus Christ. When my Lord died, he cried, "Tetelestai! It is finished!" It was a familiar word shouted by a faithful Savior about a finished work.

It has well been said that Jesus didn't make the "down payment" on the cross and then expect us to keep up the installments. Salvation isn't on the installment plan. Jesus paid it all, and that means that redemption is a finished work.

> Lifted up was He to die,
> "It is finished" was His cry;
> Now in heav'n exalted high,
> Hallelujah, what a Savior!
> (Philip P. Bliss)

Is he your Savior? He can be if you will accept his finished work on the cross, make it personal ("Christ died for my sins"), and ask Jesus to save you. "For whoever calls upon the name of the LORD shall be saved" (Joel 2:32; Acts 2:21; Rom. 10:13).

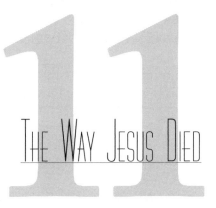

The Way Jesus Died

And when Jesus had cried out with a loud voice,
He said, "Father, into Your hands I commit My
  spirit."
Having said this, He breathed His last.

(Luke 23:46)

We are not really prepared to live unless you we prepared to die. Much of what goes on in this world is part of a continuous battle against death, but death wins in the end. Death is an appointment, not an accident, and only God knows the day and the hour when our life will end. That's why it's wonderful to be a Christian and know Jesus as your Savior, because Christians don't have to be afraid of death. Jesus' seventh statement from the cross tells us about death and how he died.

Four characteristics of his death should encourage us and remove any fear of death that may lurk in our hearts.

He Actually Died

First of all, he actually died. His death was not an illusion; he really died. The Lord Jesus had a real human body and experienced all the sinless infirmities of human nature. He knew what it was to grow up; he knew what it was to eat, drink, and sleep; he knew what it was to feel pain. And our Lord Jesus knew what it was to experience real suffering and die a real death.

The apostle John recorded that the Roman officials checked very carefully to be sure that Jesus had died. When the soldiers came to look at the bodies on the three crosses, they discovered that Jesus already was dead (see John 19:33). The soldiers broke the legs of the two thieves in order to hasten their death, but they didn't break our Lord's legs. They knew he was already dead.

When Joseph and Nicodemus asked Pilate for custody of the body of Jesus, Pilate marveled that Jesus was already dead (Mark 15:44). The official evidence of the Roman Empire was that Jesus actually died on a cross outside the city of Jerusalem. He didn't pretend to die, so he could fake a "resurrection" three days later. No, Christ died a real death on a real Roman cross, and he did it for sinners.

The evidence of the Gospel writers is that Jesus actually died. He didn't swoon on the cross and then revive when he was put into the cool tomb. The Lord Jesus Christ actually died; he tasted death for every sinner. Jesus met the last enemy—death—and defeated him!

In the Bible, the word "death" is applied to believers very infrequently; for believers, death is called "sleep." Christians who die are those who "sleep in Jesus" (1 Thess. 4:14). But when Jesus died, it wasn't sleep; it was death. He tasted the full experience of death. He confronted the last enemy with its sorrow, pain, and solemn finality. Because he died for us, we don't have to be afraid of death whenever it comes to us. "O Death, where is your sting?" (1 Cor. 15:55; see Hosea 13:14).

How grateful we should be to our Lord for going through the valley of death for us. Whether death comes to us slowly or suddenly, we know that he is with us and understands our needs. "Yea, though I walk through the valley of the shadow of death, I will fear no evil; for You are with me; Your rod and Your staff, they comfort me" (Ps. 23:4).

He Died Confidently

Jesus not only actually died, but he also died confidently. He said, "Father, into Your hands I commit my spirit" (Luke 23:46). What were the sources of our Lord's confidence as he died?

The Father's Presence

He died confidently because he had the Father's presence. He said, "Father" because he was in fellowship with his Father as his work on the cross came to an end. His cry wasn't "My God! My God!" because the darkness of separation had ended. What a wonderful thing it is to be able to look to the Father when your hour comes to leave this life.

Three times on the cross, Jesus addressed God. His first statement from the cross was "Father, forgive them, for they do not know what they do" (Luke 23:34). His fourth word was "My God, my God, why have You forsaken me?" (Matt. 27:46). His seventh word was "Father, into Your hands I commit my spirit" (Luke 23:46). At the beginning, in the middle, and at the end of his ordeal, our Lord addressed his Father.

It's worth noting that the word "Father" was often on our Lord's lips. When he was twelve years old, he said, "Did you not know that I must be about My Father's business?" (Luke 2:49). In the Sermon on the Mount, he used the word "Father" more than fifteen times. In his upper room discourse and prayer (John 13–17), our Lord mentions the Father fifty-three times. That's one reason he died confidently: he had the assurance of the Father's presence.

The Father's Promise

He died confidently because he had the Father's promise. Our Lord's last statement from the cross was a quotation from Psalm 31:5: "Into Your hand I commit my spirit; You have redeemed me, O LORD God of truth." This verse was a prayer that little Jewish boys and girls used when they retired for the night. Psalm 31:5 is an Old Testament promise, and Jesus applied it to himself. But he changed the quotation by adding a word and dropping a phrase. He is the author of the Word so he has this privilege. He added the word "Father," but he omitted the phrase "You have redeemed me, O LORD God of truth." Jesus had never sinned, so it wasn't necessary for him to be redeemed.[1] When he died, our Lord claimed God's promise and entrusted himself to his Father. That's the only way to die.

All three of the prayers from the cross are tied to Scripture. When Jesus prayed, "Father, forgive them, for they know not what they do" (Luke 23:34), he was fulfilling Isaiah 53:12: "He . . . made intercession for the transgressors." When he cried out, "My God, my God, why have You forsaken Me" (Matt. 27:46), he was quoting Psalm 22:1. When he said, "Father, into Your hands I commit My spirit" (Luke 23:46), he quoted Psalm 31:5. Our Lord Jesus lived by God's Word; if you live by God's Word, you can die by God's Word. What assurance do you have that you will experience confidence in your hour of death? The only assurance we have is the Word of God. He died confidently with the Father's presence and with the Father's promise.

The Father's Protection

Third, he had the Father's protection. "Into Your hands I commit my spirit" (Luke 23:46). For many hours our Lord had been in the hands of sinners. In the Garden of Gethsemane, he told his disciples, "The Son of Man is being betrayed into the hands of sinners" (Matt. 26:45), and the hands of sinners took hold of him and bound him. The hands of sinners beat him. The hands of sinners stripped him. The hands of sinners put a crown of thorns upon his head. The hands of sinners nailed him to a cross.

But when he came to the conclusion of his great work, Jesus Christ was no longer in the hands of sinners. He died confidently because he was in the Father's hands. The Father didn't shut him up in the hands of the enemy (Ps. 31:8). Psalm 31:15 says, "My times are in Your hand: deliver me from the hand of my enemies, and from those who persecute me." The safest place in the world is in the Father's hands.

He Died Willingly

In one sense, our Lord was killed by Roman execution-ers. Peter said, "Him . . . you have taken by lawless hands, have crucified, and put to death" (Acts 2:23). But in another sense, he was not killed, for he willingly laid down his life. He said, "Therefore My Father loves me, because I lay down My life that I may take it again. No one takes it from Me, but I lay it down of Myself. I have power to lay it down, and I have power to take it again" (John 10:17–18). Our Lord died voluntarily, the Shepherd laying down his life for the sheep.

This is an amazing thing! No Old Testament sacrifice ever died willingly. No lamb, goat, or sheep ever willingly gave its life. But Jesus willingly laid down his life for us. It's a wonderful thing to be able to say, "Father, into Your hands I commit My spirit."

Before Jesus Christ laid down his life, he forgave his ene-mies. Before he laid down his life, he gave salvation to a repentant thief. Before he laid down his life, he cared for his mother. Before he laid down his life, he finished the work God gave him to do. You and I don't know how long God will permit us to live. Every day we have, every minute we have, is a gift of his grace. But today we ought to follow Christ's example and forgive our enemies, just in case we should die. We don't want to meet the Lord with anything in our hearts against anybody. We want to come to the time of death having shared salvation with others. We want to be faithful in taking care of those who depend upon us. We want to be able to come to the end of life and surrender to God willingly, having finished the work God gave us to do.

He Died Victoriously

Finally, he died victoriously. He cried out, "Father, into Your hands I commit My spirit" (Luke 23:46). Our Lord Jesus Christ accomplished the work that God gave him to do, and when he gave up his spirit, several miracles took place. The veil of the temple was torn from top to bottom, and God opened the way into the Holy of Holies (see Matt. 27:51). Graves were opened, and some of the saints were resurrected (Matt. 27:52). Jesus Christ proved himself to be victorious over sin (the torn veil) and over death (the opened graves).

When Jesus died, an earthquake shook the area (Matt. 27:51), reminding us of the earthquake at Mount Sinai when God came down and gave the Law to Israel (see Exod. 19:18). But the earthquake at Calvary didn't announce the terror of the Law. It announced the fulfillment of the Law! The Lord Jesus Christ died victoriously, conquering sin and death and fulfilling the Law! Through him, we have victory over sin, death, and the Law. "The sting of death is sin, and the strength of sin is the law. But thanks be to God, who gives us the victory through our Lord Jesus Christ" (1 Cor. 15:56–57).

Every spiritual blessing that we have comes through the redemptive work of Christ on the cross. Every victory of faith that we win is because Jesus died for us. We overcome

Satan by the blood of the Lamb (Rev. 12:11). We enter God's presence to worship and pray because Jesus tore the veil when his flesh was torn on the cross (Heb. 10:19–22). Because we have been identified with Christ in his death, burial, and resurrection, we can overcome the flesh and walk in newness of life (Rom. 6). The world and the devil are defeated enemies because Jesus was lifted up to die on the cross (John 12:31–32). Our three great enemies—the world, the flesh, and the devil—are powerless before the cross of Jesus Christ.

Unless Jesus Christ returns to take his people to heaven, each believer will one day die. People die the way they lived. Those who live in sin will die in their sins (John 8:21). Those who live in Christ will die in Christ, safe in the Father's hands, going to the Father's house (John 14:1–6). Jesus said, "My sheep hear My voice, and I know them, and they follow Me. And I give them eternal life, and they shall never perish; neither shall anyone snatch them out of My hand" (John 10:27–28).

What a wonderful thing it is to die with confidence and assurance, able to say, "Father, into Your hands I commit my spirit." This is the heritage of the child of God.

Part 4

How Believers Should Live by the Cross

12
THE CROSS MAKES THE DIFFERENCE

The cross of Jesus Christ is much more than a symbol of the Christian faith; it's the secret of the Christian life. What was once an object of shame and scorn in the Roman world became a source of blessing and glory for those who have trusted Christ and been born again. That's why Paul could write, "But God forbid that I should glory except in the cross of our Lord Jesus Christ, by whom the world has been crucified to me, and I to the world" (Gal. 6:14).

It's the cross that makes the difference. Once you have been identified with the cross of Jesus Christ and understand some of the accomplishments of his death and resurrection, you can never be the same again. "Christ died for our sins" (1 Cor. 15:3) is a statement so simple that a child can believe it and be saved, but so profound that a theologian can never fully understand it.

Freedom

For God's people, the cross means freedom. "In Him we have redemption through His blood" (Eph. 1:7). Once we were the slaves of sin, but through his death we were set free to become the willing servants of Jesus Christ. "How shall we who died to sin live any longer in it?" asks Paul (Rom. 6:2). He gives us the answer: "But now having been set free from sin, and having become slaves of God, you have your fruit to holiness, and the end, everlasting life" (Rom. 6:22).

The theme of Romans 4 and 5 is substitution, the blessed truth that Christ took our place and died for us on the cross. He "loved me and gave Himself for me" (Gal. 2:20). But his work on the cross goes beyond substitution, as wonderful as that is. It also involves identification, which is the theme of Romans 6. Not only did Christ die for us, but we died with Christ and can say by faith, "I am crucified with Christ" (Gal. 2:20).

If you are one of God's children, then you have been identified with Christ in his death, burial, resurrection, and ascension. When he died, you died with him, and you were buried with him. When he arose, you arose with him, leaving the old life in the grave and walking "in newness of life" (Rom. 6:1–10). When he ascended, you ascended with him to sit with him on the throne of glory (Eph. 2:4–7). And when he comes again, you will appear with him in glory (Col. 3:3). From start to finish, you are identified with Jesus Christ in every victory he has won and every blessing he has gained.

Of course, these wonderful privileges bring with them great responsibilities, the first of which is to present ourselves to Christ in total surrender to him. "Present yourselves to God as being alive from the dead, and your members as instruments of righteousness to God" (Rom. 6:13). Having died with Christ, we must now reckon ourselves dead to the old life and alive in the new life. "That you put off, concerning your former conduct, the old man which grows corrupt according to the deceitful lusts, and be renewed in the spirit of your mind, and that you put on the new man which was created according to God, in true righteousness and holiness" (Eph. 4:22–24).

"Reckoning" simply means accepting as true for myself what the Bible says Jesus has done for me and acting upon it. Suppose a wealthy friend gives me a check for a thousand dollars. If I believe that he has the money in his account, then I prove my faith by endorsing the check and putting the money in my account. That's reckoning: it's acting on the basis of what God says is true about me in Jesus Christ. It's claiming for myself all that God says Christ has done for me, and acting accordingly.

In his book *The Normal Christian Life,* Watchman Nee reminds us that there were three crosses on Calvary, for two criminals were crucified along with our Lord. But how do we know that those two criminals were crucified on Golgotha? The answer is plain: God's Word tells us so. But that same Word tells us that *we* were crucified with Christ when he died on the cross! If we believe the one, why can't we believe the other and act upon it?

Jesus Christ has raised us from the dead (Eph. 2:1–7) and buried the old life forever. When Jesus raised Lazarus from the dead, he commanded, "Loose him, and let him go" (John 11:44). Lazarus was bound, so they set him free. He was wrapped in putrid graveclothes that reeked of death, but he was cleansed and given fresh garments. Why? Because he was now alive and had no need for graveclothes. He abandoned the tomb and joined the living, and the next thing you know, Lazarus is seated with Christ and bearing witness to his saving power (John 12:2, 9–11). Lazarus was now free to walk in newness of life because of Jesus Christ.

Focus

If we have identified ourselves with Christ in his Calvary victory, then our hearts and minds will have a new

125

direction as they focus heavenward. "If then you were raised with Christ, seek those things which are above, where Christ is, sitting at the right hand of God. Set your mind on things above, not on things on the earth. For you died and your life is hidden with Christ in God" (Col. 3:1–3).

You can't imagine Lazarus longing to go back to the tomb each day to live like a dead man! The son of the widow of Nain certainly wouldn't have kept his grave-clothes and the bier on which the men had carried him, nor would he gather the mourners to reenact the funeral. Living people concentrate on life, and the Christian's life is "hidden with Christ in God" (Col. 3:3). Our attention, affection, and ambition are centered in Christ "who is our life" (Col. 3:4).

When a man and woman fall in love and plan to get married, their whole outlook on life is radically changed. The pronouns change from "mine" and "yours" to "ours," and the decisions each one makes involves the other. The way they spend their time and money, the plans they make, the activities they get involved in, are all governed by one thing: we're getting married! After they've become man and wife, they maintain that same focus. Because they love each other and belong to each other, their lives are bound together, and they can't conceive of one without the other.

So it is with the believer and the Savior. Through the Holy Spirit, Christ is in us and we are in him. We can't imagine making plans or taking steps without considering his will. As we walk together with Christ, we become so united to him that we intuitively sense what will please him and what will grieve him. We seek to do only those things that please him.

Yes, the cross makes the difference between slavery to the old life and liberty in the new life, but this liberty is the liberty of obedience. "And He died for all, that those who live should live no longer for themselves, but for Him who died for them and rose again" (2 Cor. 5:15). It's the freedom of sonship, the freedom that is motivated by love and not law. "For the love of Christ compels us. . . ." (2 Cor. 5:14).

When the children of God deliberately disobey God's will, they not only rebel and commit lawlessness (1 John 3:4–7), but they also wound the heart of God. It's much more than citizens breaking the law of the king; it's children breaking the heart of their heavenly Father. Jesus was "obedient to the point of death, even the death of the cross" (Phil. 2:8), and it's unthinkable that we should come to the cross, turn our freedom into license, and willfully disobey his Word. "For you, brethren, have been called to liberty; only do not use liberty as an opportunity for the flesh. . . ." (Gal. 5:13).

Values

The dedicated believer measures everything in life by the cross. The glory of the world and every glittering offer that it makes all turn to tinsel in the light of the cross. Isaac Watts expressed it well when he wrote:

> When I survey the wondrous cross,
> On which the prince of glory died,
> My richest gain I count but loss,
> And pour contempt on all my pride.
> Forbid it, Lord, that I should boast,
> Save in the death of Christ my God;
> All the vain things that charm me most,
> I sacrifice them to His blood.

When measured by the cross, no sacrifice we make is too great, no amount of suffering we endure is too unbearable, no burden we carry is too heavy, and no assignment we receive from God is too difficult. The glory of the cross cuts man's glory down to size and reduces man's pride to a mere puff of wind.

The fleshly ambitions and achievements of the Christ-rejecting world become but garbage at the foot of the cross. "For what is highly esteemed among men is an abomination in the sight of God" (Luke 16:15).

Peter counseled our Lord not to go to the cross (Matt. 16:21–23), and the crowd told him to come down from the cross (Matt. 27:40–44). Our Lord resisted both temptations and so must we. "If anyone desires to come after Me, let him deny himself, and take up his cross, and follow Me" (Matt. 16:24).

> Must Jesus bear the cross alone,
> And all the world go free?
> No, there's a cross for everyone,
> And there's a cross for me.

Referring to the experience of Simon of Cyrene, who carried our Lord's cross (Matt. 27:32), Thomas Shepherd's original lines were:

> Shall Simon bear the cross alone,
> And other saints be free?
> Each saint of Thine shall find his own,
> And there is one for me.

Bearing the cross is not a metaphor for experiencing the normal human difficulties of life, such as living or working with disagreeable people or having to put up with difficult circumstances. Even unsaved people have to do that. To bear his cross daily means to be identified with Christ in his shame, suffering, and death; to be treated the way he was treated because we obey God as he obeyed; to die to self and live by faith so that God's will is accomplished on earth.

But when we bear the cross, we save our lives. "For whoever desires to save his life will lose it, but whoever loses his life for My sake will find it" (Matt. 16:25). A crossless life is a wasted life. No matter how much enjoyment we experience or accomplishment we achieve, without the cross our lives have been fruitless and in vain. "Most assuredly, I say to you, unless a grain of wheat falls into the ground and dies, it remains alone; but if it dies, it produces much grain. He who loves his life will lose it, and he who hates his life in this world will keep it for eternal life" (John 12:24–25).

Imagine coming to the end of your life, looking back, and discovering that all those years were wasted! And you can't have the opportunity to live them again! You gained what you wanted from the world, but you lost your life, and now life is over. Paradoxically, bearing the cross of Christ involves both death and life, loss and gain, suffering and glory. The seed is planted in the earth and dies, but it brings forth beauty and fruitfulness. Jim Elliot expressed it perfectly when on October 28, 1949, he wrote in his journal, "He is no fool who gives what he cannot keep to gain what he cannot lose."

Endurance

Jesus endured the cross because of "the joy that was set before Him" (Heb. 12:2), the joy of returning to his Father in heaven (John 17:3), and one day presenting his church before the throne of God in glory (John 17:24; Jude 24). He was able to endure the present because he was certain about the future.

Paul had a similar outlook on the Christian life. "Even though our outward man is perishing, yet the inward man is being renewed day by day. For our light affliction, which is but for a moment, is working for us a far more exceeding and eternal weight of glory" (2 Cor. 4:16–17). "For I consider that the sufferings of this present time are not worthy to be compared with the glory which shall be revealed in us" (Rom. 8:18).

And Peter had the same philosophy of life. "In this you greatly rejoice, though now for a little while, if need be, you have been grieved by various trials, that the genuineness of your faith, being much more precious than gold that perishes, though it is tested by fire, may be found to praise, honor, and glory at the revelation of Jesus Christ" (1 Peter 1:6–7). Peter had resisted the cross because he thought that such shameful suffering was beneath the dignity of the Savior, but then he learned that the cross was the doorway to Christ's glory.

It's one thing to wear a cross hanging on a gold chain or pinned to the lapel, but it's quite another thing to bear a cross and follow Jesus in his shame, suffering, and death. "If anyone serves Me, let him follow Me; and where I am, there will My servant be also. If anyone serves Me, him My Father will honor" (John 12:26). Paul called this "the fellowship of His sufferings" (Phil. 3:10).

We come to the cross by faith to find eternal salvation, and we carry the cross by faith to experience daily sanctification and satisfaction. We die to that which is out of God's will so that we might enjoy all that is in his will, and we don't consider ourselves making much of a sacrifice, at least not when it's compared to what Jesus did for us.

When we Christians are truly cross bearers, we find ourselves unconcerned about the world's offers of pleasure and success but greatly concerned about the world's need for a Savior. We don't have time to fuss with the saints over who is the greatest in the church, because we're too consumed with Christ's glory to be distracted by man's praise. Our priorities are worship and service, witness and sacrifice, all to the glory of God. Regardless of how much Demas offers us in this present world (2 Tim. 4:10), we have no desire to join him.

The embarrassing problems that exist among God's people in the churches would be quickly solved if all of us were cross bearers. To the "mature" saints in the Roman assemblies who were despising their overscrupulous brethren, Paul wrote, "Do not destroy with your food the one for whom Christ died" (Rom. 14:15); and he asked the competitive, divisive Corinthians, "Was Paul crucified for you?" (1 Cor. 1:13).

The saints in the Galatian churches were biting and devouring each other, so Paul reminded them to glory in the cross and not in their religious accomplishments (Gal. 6:11–15). He admonished Christian husbands in Ephesus to love their wives "just as Christ also loved the church and gave Himself for her" (Eph. 5:25). When he wrote to the Philippians about the worldly believers in their midst, he wept and called them "the enemies of the cross of Christ" (Phil. 3:18). He told the believers in Colosse who were enamored of Jewish religious rituals that the law was taken out of the way because Jesus nailed it to his cross (Col. 2:14).

In short, there's no personal or doctrinal problem that can't be solved if we take it to Calvary. Perhaps the embarrassing divisions and disputes among professed Christians today are evidence of the fact that the cross of Jesus Christ is no longer preeminent in our worship, theology, or daily walk.

Progress

Saintly Samuel Rutherford, who endured much for the cause of Christ, wrote that the cross "is such a burden as sails are to a ship or wings to a bird." In this statement, he wasn't denying the pain or the price of faithful discipleship, because Rutherford experienced too much to promote that kind of an illusion. Rather, he was affirming what the saints of God have always affirmed, that bearing the cross is the only means of certain progress in the Christian life.

A modern saint, F. J. Huegel, wrote: "The Cross does not lead to passivity. It does not crucify any faculty. On the contrary, it releases powers we never dreamed we possessed. . . . We are cast again and again into the mould of the Cross—being made conformable to Christ's death."[1]

"There are no crown-wearers in heaven who were not crossbearers here below," said Charles Haddon Spurgeon. To quote Isaac Watts again:

> But drops of grief can ne'er repay
> The debt of love I owe;
> Here, Lord, I give myself away—
> 'Tis all that I can do.

Notes

Chapter 1

1. Weatherhead, Leslie. *The Will of God* (Nashville: Abingdon-Cokesbury Press, 1944), p. 12.

2. Gramatically speaking, the Greek text permits the phrase "from the creation of the world" to be applied either to "have not been written" or "that was slain." Most commentators apply it to the latter phrase.

Chapter 2

1. My statements about these two neighborhoods are generalizations. There were certainly vulgar people living among the cultured crowd in the "Gold Coast" and cultured people living in "Old Town." Every large city has these typical neighborhoods.

Chapter 4

1. Price, Lucien, ed., *Dialogues of Alfred North Whitehead* (Boston: Little, Brown and Co., 1954), p. 277.

2. Lewis, C. S., *Christian Behaviour* (New York: Macmillan, 1946), p. 55.

3. *Metropolitan Tabernacle Pulpit,* vol. 22, p. 599.

Chapter 8

1. Note that David also wrote about our Lord's resurrection in verses 22–31. See Hebrews 2:10–12.

Chapter 10

1. The suggestion for this approach comes from *A Handful of Stars* by F. W. Boreham (Judson Press, 1950), p. 104.

Chapter 11

1. Of course, this "redemption" could be applied to his resurrection from the dead. When David wrote Psalm 31, he was concerned about being redeemed from his enemies.

Chapter 12

1. Huegel., F. J., *The Cross of Christ—the Throne of God* (Minneapolis: Bethany Fellowship, 1965), p. 141.

Warren W. Wiersbe is Distinguished Professor of Preaching at Grand Rapids Baptist Seminary and has pastored churches in Indiana, Kentucky, and Illinois (Chicago's historic Moody Church). He is the author of more than 100 books, including *God Isn't in a Hurry,* *The Bumps Are What You Climb On,* and *The Bible Exposition Commentary* (2 vols.).